21 Benefits of Being a Believer:

Devotional & Scripture Reference

Terell Ward

Manufactured in the United States of America

ISBN 978-1-62590-021-0

Book Cover Design: Jalana Houston

Editor: Daphne Parsekian

DEDICATION

And

ACKNOWLEDGMENTS

This book is dedicated to my family: my wonderful wife, Ebonique; my two sons, Elias and Zion; and my father, Tommy Ward. This book is also dedicated all of my Sunday school teachers, ministers and Pastors who have poured into my life over the years.

Table of Contents

INTRODUCTION

As believers, the greatest asset we have is God's Word, and on His Word is where we place our faith and total trust. God's Word is our health, strength, guidance, peace, joy, deliverance, and salvation. The Word of God is the answer to all of life's problems and situations; it shades light to darkness and brings truth to light in our lives. But many believers do not read God's Word daily, and studies have shown that most Christians in the USA rarely read their Bible at all. This information brings light to the fact that many Christians do not walk in the promises God has for them simply because they don't know they have them. If you don't know that something belongs to you, you will never ask for it or expect it.

I have spent most of my life in church, and I have seen believers run through the church praising God, speaking in tongues, and just about doing a cartwheel giving God glory, but their lives outside of the church didn't bring God much glory. They lived in poverty, bondage from addictions, and ultimate defeat. And as a young person, I always wondered how they could be saved and read all of the promises God says in His Word and not experience them in their lives. How was it that their lives reflected everything other than what the Word of God says a born again believer's life should reflect? As I grew older, I learned the answers to my youthful questions. I learned that some of the people were in the midst of a storm, that their present circumstance was only for a moment, and God, as He promised, would turn their situation around. But, unfortunately, there were far less of these testimonies than I expected. What I also found out was that most people did not get to see the fulfillment of their blessings from God. This was caused by many different reasons, but the top two were their own decision not to live for God totally and, most important, that they NEVER opened their Bible outside of Sunday

1

service. As a result, I saw many believers failing in life because of their lack of knowledge, which God says will happen to us if we don't study His Word (Hosea 4:6).

While counseling believers, I found that many people did not even know what the Bible promised them. They did not know that God desires that they live prosperously in every area of their lives (3 John 1:2). If we live in the dark about the rights and power that we have, we will never be able to appropriate them. I was like many believers during a time in my life in which I had power and privilege because I was a son of God but I never applied my privilege and ultimately settled for less than the best. I like to use the following example when I am preaching of this scenario: Imagine a person who is living day by day, just trying to make it. He is barely getting by, and every time something goes wrong, he finds himself deeper in the hole he found himself in prior to the unfortunate turn of events. But he had a father who was a billionaire who left him an inheritance. His father put his inheritance in a bank, and the father gave his son the bank card and told him what bank his inheritance was in. The only responsibility the son had was open a letter his father had left for him to read at the time of his death, which contained the pin number to the bank card so he could access his inheritance. Now, many of you are probably thinking that this is a no brainer. The son will obviously read the letter his dad left, get the pin number, and head straight to the bank to get his money! But this son never opens the letter; he puts it away in his drawer or he buys a picture frame for it and puts it up in his house as a decorative item. He never reads the letter, so he never gets access to his inheritance. His father worked hard to leave his son a great opportunity for the future, but the son chose to try to handle it all on his own. This story makes the son seem like an unintelligent guy to say the least, because all the son had to do was read the letter and his life would be changed for the better forever. I know all of you reading this are saying you would never make this mistake, but most

2

of us do each day. Many believers do not open their Bibles, and they are just like the son in the story; they have the answer to their problems tucked away in their dresser drawers or nicely displayed in their living room, but they never actually read it. God promises us that the plans He has for us are to prosper us and give us hope and that we will have a successful future (Jeremiah 29:11), but we will never know this if we don't open our Bibles.

I was led by the Lord to write this book, because during my time of counseling people I found that many people want to know what God's promises are for them. Unfortunately, they don't read their Bibles because they did not know where to start or they couldn't find what they were looking for. The Bible is a big book, and it can be difficult to find the exact answer you were looking for from God. So, my job here on earth is to help point people in the right direction. This book will give you countless verses that I have found throughout the Bible that will give you God's answers to life's problems. The Bible is our constitution as Kingdom Citizens, and it is important that we learn our rights as citizens so they we can properly appropriate them. Knowing your Bible is not just important for you to have knowledge of Scriptures, but it will benefit your prayer life, marriage, parenting, finances, and every area of your life. It is important to note here that just memorizing Bible verses is not the key to access of the benefits, but actually applying them to your life is. In the example of the son with the inheritance, it would have not done him any good if he had read the letter from his father and never went to the bank to receive his inheritance. The son not only needed the pin code but he needed to take action with this knowledge in order for it to benefit him. The same is true of us as believers; we have to first learn what God promises us and then apply the Scriptures to our lives to see the results. This is a key point for us to understand before we begin to explore the Scriptures so that we can have the right type of mindset while studying.

Studying the Bible also gives the believer the correct prospective on life. We learned from the Word of God that we live by faith and not by sight (2 Corinthians 5:7). What this means as a believer is that however we may feel about how life is going, or whether the situations in our life may seem crazy and out of control, God's Word is the *reality* of our lives. We are supposed to live according to what God's Word says about us and how life should be viewed. We do not live life guided by our feelings or how things appear to be. I remember this point being driven home in my life when I saw a preacher put his Bible in front of his face and say, "This is how we should view our lives." His point was that we need to put on *spiritual* glasses when looking at life. Everything we go through should be analyzed with God's Word. We need to learn how to see things as God sees them and not according to what our financial advisors, family members, and news media portray them to be. God gives us this ability when we are born again, and it is strengthened every time we open our Bible to study and meditate on His Word. We begin to get a clearer understanding of God's will for our lives and how He does things. Now, the Bible does say that God's ways are above our ways and His thoughts are not our thoughts (Isaiah 55:8), but as we study our Bibles, He will reveal Himself to us if we seek Him with all of our heart (Jeremiah 29:13). And when it does come to those moments when we can't seem to hear God or get an understanding of what He is doing, that's when we stand strong in our faith of who He is as our God. We put our trust in the fact that He said He would never leave us or forsake us (Hebrews 13:5 & Deuteronomy 31:6) and that He promised to never put more on us than we can bear (1 Corinthians 10:13).

As you are using this book as a resource, make sure that you are not just spending time reading Bible verses but that you are taking the time to meditate on the Word. I encourage you to get into a quiet place when you are studying so that all the outside distractions are removed

4

from your presence. Then you can speak to the Lord in prayer, and you will be in a place where you can hear Him speak through His Spirit back to you. God desires great things for your life; He created you to accomplish them! Remember to always see yourself as God sees you and never forget that you are special and destined for greatness!

Let's get started!

Dominion

Genesis 1:26-28 — And God said, Let us make man in our image, after our likeness: and let them have

dominion over the fish of the sea, and over the fowl of the air, and over the cattle, and over all the earth,

and over every creeping thing that creepeth upon the earth. [27] So God created man in his own image, in

the image of God created he him; male and female created he them. [28] And God blessed them, and God said

unto them, Be fruitful, and multiply, and replenish the earth, and subdue it: and have dominion over the

fish of the sea, and over the fowl of the air, and over every living thing that moveth upon the earth. (KJV)

God is a God of purpose. Everything God created He created with a specific purpose in mind. The Bible teaches us also that God's purposes do not change. Understanding this fact brings confidence to us as believers, because as we discover what God's purpose is for us as mankind and individually, we can have a sense of direction in life and confidence. God's original purpose for mankind was to have **dominion** over the earth (Genesis 1:26-28). This is the reason why every human on earth spends their whole life in one way or another chasing after power, money, or fame. Why? Because these things bring a sense of control, authority, or *dominion*. The desire for dominion over our environment is a natural desire from God. Why? Because God's purpose was for mankind to *have* dominion over the earth and not the earth having dominion over mankind!

If we want to get a good picture of God's original purpose, we do not have to go further than Genesis chapters 1 and 2. These are the two chapters before the fall of mankind due to the sin of Adam and man's need for a savior. These chapters reveal to us God's perfect creation and His original purpose for all of His creation. In Genesis 1:26-28 we find the creation of man and woman and what God desired for us in regards to our role here on earth. God purposed for us to be fruitful, multiply, replenish the earth, subdue the earth, and to have dominion. The word dominion here translated in its original Hebrew form means royal authority, and kingdom. God purposed us to live as kings on the earth! One key point to understand about a king is that wherever his kingdom was, he had complete control over it. God wanted us to control our environment through the authority that He bestowed upon us from the beginning.

This is the very reason why people fight for money so hard. Money, along with other things, brings a sense of control. When someone has a lot of money, they can use their money to control their environment much more than someone who does not have money. They can buy the material things they want, they can pick where they want to live, and they can do what they want to do when they want to do it, unlike the person who does not have a lot of money. This person is told what they can or cannot have, they are told where they can live, and they do not get to choose what they want to do for themselves most of the time. There is a sense of dominion in having great wealth. But money can't buy everything, and if a person falls in love with money, it will consume their whole life and leave them deprived of the many other blessings God desires for them. As believers, we have the benefit of being able to walk once again in our kingly dominion on this earth when we became born again. God restores the right we had from His original purpose to live a life of victory and not defeat! We are now empowered by the Holy Spirit to walk in our dominion each day, and nothing in this world has the power or right to dominate us **ever** again!

Being a believer put us back in line with God's original purpose, and we have the right to walk in dominion power. Nothing and no one should control us but God through the Holy Spirit and His Word (Bible). As you study the Scriptures on your dominion power, remember to speak the Word of God over your life daily. Meditate on God's Word, and allow the Holy Spirit to lead you in the knowledge of your dominion.

Do you control your environment? Or does your environment control you?

Dominion Scriptures

(Genesis 1:26 ESV) Then God said, "Let us make man in our image, after our likeness. And let them have dominion over the fish of the sea and over the birds of the heavens and over the livestock and over all the earth and over every creeping thing that creeps on the earth."

(Genesis 1:28 ESV) And God blessed them. And God said to them, "Be fruitful and multiply and fill the earth and subdue it and have dominion over the fish of the sea and over the birds of the heavens and over every living thing that moves on the earth."

(Romans 6:14 ESV) For sin will have no dominion over you, since you are not under law but under grace.

(Luke 10:19 ESV) Behold, I have given you authority to tread on serpents and scorpions, and over all the power of the enemy, and nothing shall hurt you.

(1 John 3:2 ESV) Beloved, we are God's children now, and what we will be has not yet appeared; but we know that when he appears we shall be like him, because we shall see him as he is.

(Psalm 8:6 ESV) You have given him dominion over the works of your hands; you have put all things under his feet,

(1 Peter 3:18 ESV) For Christ also suffered once for sins, the righteous for the unrighteous, that he might bring us to God, being put to death in the flesh but made alive in the spirit,

(Romans 5:17 ESV) For if, because of one man's trespass, death reigned through that one man, much more will those who receive the abundance of grace and the free gift of righteousness reign in life through the one man Jesus Christ..

(Colossians 2:14 ESV) By canceling the record of debt that stood against us with its legal demands. This he set aside, nailing it to the cross.

(Acts 17:30-31 ESV) The times of ignorance God overlooked, but now he commands all people everywhere to repent, because he has fixed a day on which he will judge the world in righteousness by a man whom he has appointed; and of this he has given assurance to all by raising him from the dead."

(Acts 3:19-21 ESV) Repent therefore, and turn again, that your sins may be blotted out, that times of refreshing may come from the presence of the Lord, and that he may send the Christ appointed for you, Jesus, whom heaven must receive until the time for restoring all the things about which God spoke by the mouth of his holy prophets long ago.

(Luke 3:16-17 ESV) John answered them all, saying, "I baptize you with water, but he who is mightier than I is coming, the strap of whose sandals I am not worthy to untie. He will baptize you with the Holy Spirit and with fire. His winnowing fork is in his hand, to clear his threshing floor and to gather the wheat into his barn, but the chaff he will burn with unquenchable fire."

(Mark 5:1-20 ESV) They came to the other side of the sea, to the country of the Gerasenes. [2] And when Jesus had stepped out of the boat, immediately there met him out of the tombs a man with an unclean spirit.[3] He lived among the tombs. And no one could bind him anymore, not even with a chain, [4] for he had often been bound with shackles and chains, but he wrenched the chains apart, and he broke the shackles in pieces. No one had the strength to subdue him. [5] Night and day among the tombs and on the mountains he was always crying out and cutting himself with stones. [6] And when he saw Jesus from afar, he ran and fell down before him. [7] And crying out with a loud voice, he said, "What have you to do with me, Jesus, Son of the Most High God? I adjure you by God, do not torment me." [8] For he was saying to him, "Come out of the man, you unclean spirit!" [9] And Jesus asked him, "What is your name?" He replied, "My name is Legion, for we are many." [10] And he begged him earnestly not to send them out of the country. [11] Now a great herd of pigs was feeding there on the hillside, [12] and they begged him, saying, "Send us to the pigs; let us enter them." [13] So he gave them permission. And the unclean spirits came out and entered the pigs; and the herd, numbering about two thousand, rushed down the steep bank into the sea and drowned in the sea. [14] The herdsmen fled and told it in the city and in the country. And people came to see what it was that had happened. [15] And they came to Jesus and saw the demon-possessed man, the one who had had the legion, sitting there, clothed and in his right mind, and they were afraid. [16] And those who had seen it described to them what had happened to the demon-possessed man and to the pigs.[17] And they began to beg Jesus[d] to depart from their region. [18] As he was getting into the boat, the man who had been possessed with demons begged him that he might be with him. [19] And he did not permit him but said to him, "Go home to your friends and tell them how much the Lord has done for you, and how he has had mercy on you." [20] And he went away and began to proclaim in the Decapolis how much Jesus had done for him, and everyone marveled.

(John 12:30-32 ESV) Jesus answered, "This voice has come for your sake, not mine. [31] Now is the judgment of this world; now will the ruler of this world be cast out.[32] And I, when I am lifted up from the earth, will draw all people to myself."

(Matthew 24:42 ESV) Therefore, stay awake, for you do not know on what day your Lord is coming.

(Matthew 24:36 ESV) "But concerning that day and hour no one knows, not even the angels of heaven, nor the Son, but the Father only.

(Acts 2:38 ESV) And Peter said to them, "Repent and be baptized every one of you in the name of Jesus Christ for the forgiveness of your sins, and you will receive the gift of the Holy Spirit.

Healing

Isaiah 53:5 — But he was pierced for our transgressions, he was crushed for our iniquities; the punishment that brought us peace was on him, and by his wounds we are healed.(NIV)

Sickness and disease are major problems facing our world today. Many people suffer every day with pain in their bodies or watch family and friends go through tough times with their health. Our technology has grown, and modern medicine has taken major steps toward different treatments and drugs, but we are far from totally ridding our world of sickness. As much effort as the doctors and scientists of the world put towards cures, they will never be able to keep up with the complicity of viruses in our world. With this knowledge in mind, the future could seem dark; with all our efforts, we still could come up short in the area of our health.

As believers, we have a hope that supersedes what our doctors and scientists are capable of doing. We are not supposed to put our faith in them but in what God says. The Word of God says in Isaiah 53:5 *"by His stripes we are healed"* (NKJV). Jesus Christ came to earth to restore mankind back to his rightful place with God, and along with making eternal life available to us, He also restored our God-given right to be in good health while here on earth. God never desired for disease to grip the earth and for it to destroy the lives of mankind and wildlife, but when sin came onto the earth through the fall of man in Genesis 3 so did disease and all kinds of sickness. But the good news is that God is a God who stays true to His Word (Numbers 23:19). Even though mankind allowed sickness into the world, God did not want it and sent His son to bring us out of the bondage of it.

In Isaiah 53:5, we see that the Word of the Lord says that the stripes Jesus took for us released God's healing power over our lives. Jesus paid the price for our sins and for the healing over our bodies! This is a great fact for us to remember as believers, because whenever we get sick, the first person we should tell about it is our heavenly Father. God's Word tells us here in Isaiah that the beating Jesus took gave us our right to live healthy lives. The Bible tells us that He was beaten to the point of not being recognized (Isaiah 52:13-15). He took on this type of pain in His body so that we could be redeemed from pain in our bodies! We deserved to be sick and live in pain because of our sin, but God stays true to His Word regardless of our actions. And as believers, when we accepted Jesus Christ as our Lord and Savior, good health became our right. Everything that God promised in His Word became a part of our inheritance as children of God. It does not matter if the illness we are going through was caused by our own doing; as children of God, we have the right to go to God to ask for healing to be restored in our bodies. God, not being a respecter of man, will hear our prayers for healing because of what His Son did for us. Because we have accepted His Son as our Lord and Savior, we have a full inheritance of healing that is due to us!

If you are sick or know of someone who is sick, remind them of this scripture. Remember that Jesus paid the price in His body for our mistakes, and we now have the privilege of being healed. It does not matter how bad you may think you have been; Jesus restored your health thousands of years ago, and all you have to do is have faith in what He's already done! Start speaking to your body that you **ARE** healed, because that is what the Word says (Isaiah 53:5). The key words to this scripture are: *are healed*. The Bible does not say we will become or we will soon be. Why is this? Why doesn't the Bible say we will become healed? The reason is because when Jesus came to earth and took a humiliating beating for us and died on the cross, He sealed our futures in the spirit realm. Once we are born again, the transformation that takes place in our lives starts with our spirit man and then it is manifested in our natural

14

bodies and lives. So, when we get sick, we can pray to God and remind God of what Jesus did and that we have the right to be healed, and God will begin to manifest healing in our natural bodies. Our healing can happen immediately or over a course of time. Our job is to believe God that He will stand by His Word and heal us, and the length of time that He chooses is His prerogative. Our job is to stand on His Word that He will do it for us.

As you start to study the many scriptures pertaining to healing in the Bible, make sure you memorize them and keep them constantly on your mind throughout your day. Keep reminding yourself that you are a child of God, and healing is your right! Speak God's Word over yourself continuously, and watch how God will manifest it in your body or the body of those you are praying for.

What do you or your family need God to heal? How can you spread the message of God's healing power to your family and friends?

Healing Scriptures

(2 Chronicles 7:14 NKJV) "If My people who are called by My name will humble themselves, and pray and seek My face, and turn from their wicked ways, then I will hear from heaven, and will forgive their sin and heal their land.

(Psalms 30:2 NKJV) O LORD my God, I cried out to You, And You healed me.

(Psalms 103:1-4 NKJV) Bless the LORD, O my soul; And all that is within me, bless His holy name! {2} Bless the LORD, O my soul, And forget not all His benefits: {3} Who forgives all your iniquities, Who heals all your diseases, {4} Who redeems your life from destruction, Who crowns you with lovingkindness and tender mercies,

(Psalms 107:20 NKJV) He sent His word and healed them, And delivered them from their destructions.

(Psalms 147:3 NKJV) He heals the brokenhearted And binds up their wounds.

(Proverbs 3:7-8 NKJV) Do not be wise in your own eyes; Fear the LORD and depart from evil. {8} It will be health to your flesh, And strength to your bones.

(Proverbs 4:20-22 NKJV) My son, give attention to my words; Incline your ear to my sayings. {21} Do not let them depart from your eyes; Keep them in the midst of your heart; {22} For they are life to those who find them, And health to all their flesh.

(Isaiah 53:5 NKJV) But He was wounded for our transgressions, He was bruised for our iniquities; The chastisement for our peace was upon Him, And by His stripes we are healed.

(Isaiah 58:8 NKJV) Then your light shall break forth like the morning, Your healing shall spring forth speedily, And your righteousness shall go before you; The glory of the LORD shall be your rear guard.

(Isaiah 61:1 NKJV) "The Spirit of the Lord GOD is upon Me, Because the LORD has anointed Me To preach good tidings to the poor; He has sent Me to heal the brokenhearted, To proclaim liberty to the captives, And the opening of the prison to those who are bound;

(Jeremiah 3:22 NKJV) "Return, you backsliding children, And I will heal your backslidings." "Indeed we do come to You, For You are the LORD our God.

(Jeremiah 17:14 NKJV) Heal me, O LORD, and I shall be healed; Save me, and I shall be saved, For You are my praise.

(Jeremiah 30:17 NKJV) For I will restore health to you And heal you of your wounds,' says the LORD, 'Because they called you an outcast saying: "This is Zion; No one seeks her."'

(Jeremiah 33:6 NKJV) 'Behold, I will bring it health and healing; I will heal them and reveal to them the abundance of peace and truth.

(Malachi 4:2 NKJV) But to you who fear My name The Sun of Righteousness shall arise With healing in His wings; And you shall go out And grow fat like stall-fed calves.

(Matthew 4:23 NKJV) And Jesus went about all Galilee, teaching in their synagogues, preaching the gospel of the kingdom, and healing all kinds of sickness and all kinds of disease among the people.

(Matthew 8:13 NKJV) Then Jesus said to the centurion, "Go your way; and as you have believed, so let it be done for you." And his servant was healed that same hour.

(Matthew 8:16 NKJV) When evening had come, they brought to Him many who were demon-possessed. And He cast out the spirits with a word, and healed all who were sick,

(Matthew 9:35 NKJV) Then Jesus went about all the cities and villages, teaching in their synagogues, preaching the gospel of the kingdom, and healing every sickness and every disease among the people.

(Matthew 10:1 NKJV) And when He had called His twelve disciples to Him, He gave them power over unclean spirits, to cast them out, and to heal all kinds of sickness and all kinds of disease.

(Matthew 10:8 NKJV) "Heal the sick, cleanse the lepers, raise the dead, cast out demons. Freely you have received, freely give.

(Matthew 12:22 NKJV) Then one was brought to Him who was demon-possessed, blind and mute; and He healed him, so that the blind and mute man both spoke and saw.

(Matthew 14:14 NKJV) And when Jesus went out He saw a great multitude; and He was moved with compassion for them, and healed their sick.

(Luke 6:19 NKJV) And the whole multitude sought to touch Him, for power went out from Him and healed them all.

(Luke 9:6 NKJV) So they departed and went through the towns, preaching the gospel and healing everywhere.(The twelve are sent out)

(Luke 10:8-9 NKJV) "Whatever city you enter, and they receive you, eat such things as are set before you. {9} "And heal the sick there, and say to them, 'The kingdom of God has come near to you.

(Luke 17:15 NKJV) And one of them, when he saw that he was healed, returned, and with a loud voice glorified God,

(Acts 3:12 NKJV) So when Peter saw it, he responded to the people: "Men of Israel, why do you marvel at this? Or why look so intently at us, as though by our own power or godliness we had made this man walk?

(Acts 4:29-31 NKJV) "Now, Lord, look on their threats, and grant to Your servants that with all boldness they may speak Your word, {30} "by stretching out Your hand to heal, and that signs and wonders may be done through the name of Your holy Servant Jesus." {31} And when they had prayed, the place where they were assembled together was shaken; and they were all filled with the Holy Spirit, and they spoke the word of God with boldness.

(1 Corinthians 12:9 NKJV) to another faith by the same Spirit, to another gifts of healings by the same Spirit,

(James 5:14-16 NKJV) Is anyone among you sick? Let him call for the elders of the church, and let them pray over him, anointing him with oil in the name of the Lord. {15} And the prayer of faith will save the sick, and the Lord will raise him up. And if he has committed sins, he will be forgiven. {16} Confess your trespasses to one another, and pray for one another, that you may be healed. The effective, fervent prayer of a righteous man avails much.

(Luke 8:47-48 NKJV) Now when the woman saw that she was not hidden, she came trembling; and falling down before Him, she declared to Him in the presence of all the people the reason she had touched Him and how she was healed immediately. And He said to her, "Daughter, be of good cheer; your faith has made you well. Go in peace."

(Luke 5:17 NKJV) Now it happened on a certain day, as He was teaching, that there were Pharisees and teachers of the law sitting by, who had come out of every town of Galilee, Judea, and Jerusalem. And the power of the Lord was present to heal them.

Peace

Philippians 4:7 — And the peace of God, which transcends all understanding, will guard your hearts

and your minds in Christ Jesus. (NIV)

Peace is something that countries go to war to try to achieve; people spend millions of dollars each year on vacations, material things, and other outlets to bring some type of peace to their world. Every human being desires to have peace, but few really experience it. What is peace? By definition, peace is defined as, *"the normal, non-warring condition of a nation, group of nations, or the world."* It is *also* defined as, *"cessation of or freedom from any strife or dissension."* As we can see here from the definition of peace from our dictionaries, we as a human race rarely have ever lived in peace. From the beginning of time, we found civilizations at war with each other, and even today many of the world's countries are at war or on the verge of it.

Our fight for peace has not been able to bring about what we are fighting for. But God says that He will give us peace. How is this possible? How can God give us peace when we are constantly at war with each other and there is civil unrest? Does it mean that God will end all wars and everyone will start to love each other? Unfortunately, as much as we would love to see this happen, it will not. So, the question becomes, what did God mean when He said in His Word that He would give us peace that surpassed all of our understanding (Philippians 4:7).

I believe we first have to redefine what God calls peace. God's peace is not the same as what the world considers peace. The world says peace is no wars, no calamity, or no conflict, but God's peace has nothing to do with the circumstances or environment. God's peace is comfort in the time of trouble; it is rest in the time of storms. God's peace is what keeps us calm

20

when the world around us is out of control; it is how we can continue to function with our everyday lives when all hell has broken loose in our homes, on our jobs, and in our communities.

The Bible says that God's peace surpasses or exceeds our understanding, which means we never really will be able to understand it, but we have the right to experience it each and every day of our lives. This peace stems from the fact that God is always in control, and no matter what the circumstances look like, we are going to be all right.

Remember the story of Jesus and disciples on the boat in (Mark 4:35-40). They were on the boat, and a great storm came and the wind and waves started to damage the boat. The disciples were terrified, but Jesus was asleep while all this was happening. His disciples eventually came and asked Him if He cared about them, because they feared that the ship was about to go down; He seemed like He was going to allow it to happen, because He was asleep. Jesus teaches us a good lesson about peace in this passage of Scripture. Before they took off, Jesus said to His disciples that *they were going to go to the other side*" (Mark 4:35). At that moment their fate was set, because Jesus had spoken their future. He told them that their journey would end with all of them on the other side. So Jesus, knowing what He said, was at peace and decided to go to sleep. I believe that Jesus knew a storm was coming; He also knew how bad the storm was going to be and what it was going to do to their boat. But He could be at peace, because He knew He was going to make it to the other side! Jesus was teaching us that in God's peace we can sleep like a baby through a storm; if God said something was going to happen in our lives, all we have to do is put our faith in it and ride the storms of life out.

They have a saying in my childhood church that says, "Storms don't last always." When Jesus told them they were going to the other side, all the disciples could have gone to sleep with

Jesus! This is why, once they woke Jesus up, the first thing He said to them was, *"Why are you so fearful?"* (Mark 4:40). And then He goes on to say in the second part of the verse, *"How is it that you have no faith?"*

Let's look closely here at the fact that Jesus said they were operating in fear rather than faith. Fear will always destroy your faith, which will remove God's peace in your life. God's peace is based on our faith in God. When we have faith in God's Word, God's peace is allowed to take over our minds and positions us to function in the midst of a storm. When we put our trust in God, something begins to happen that we can't explain about our mindsets and perspectives on life.

I have seen people with cancer, paralyzed in their body for life, or living with HIV live in more peace than young adults who are financially stable and healthy, who have their whole lives still ahead of them. The difference between these people is the peace that comes from God and not man. God's peace comforts the person whose body is racked with pain or those living so far below the poverty line that they don't know when their next meal is going to come. I have watched these people put their trust in God's Word and live in peace while they waited on the Lord. The best part about their stories is that God provided for each and every one of their needs! They trusted God and experienced true peace in their lives.

As you are studying the scriptures on peace, remember to ask God to remove all the fear, anxiety, and stress from your mind so that you can receive His peace. God promised us His peace because we are His children. He cares not only that we get through the storms of life, but He is extremely concerned with *how* we come through them as well. Remember to speak the Word of God over your life daily in the areas where you want to see God make a change (which should be every area).

Are you truly experiencing God's peace in your life? If not, why?

Peace Scriptures

(Psalm 119:165 NIV) Great peace have they who love your law, and nothing can make them stumble.

(Isaiah 9:6 NIV) For to us a child is born, to us a son is given, and the government will be on his shoulders. And he will be called Wonderful Counselor, Mighty God, Everlasting Father, Prince of Peace.

(Isaiah 26:3 NIV) You will keep in perfect peace him whose mind is steadfast, because he trusts in you.

(Isaiah 26:12 NIV) LORD, you establish peace for us; all that we have accomplished you have done for us.

(Isaiah 54:10 NIV) Though the mountains be shaken and the hills be removed, yet my unfailing love for you will not be shaken nor my covenant of peace be removed," says the LORD, who has compassion on you.

(Isaiah 55:12 NIV) You will go out in joy and be led forth in peace; the mountains and hills will burst into song before you, and all the trees of the field will clap their hands.

(Matthew 11:28-30 NIV) "Come to me, all you who are weary and burdened, and I will give you rest. Take my yoke upon you and learn from me, for I am gentle and humble in heart, and you will find rest for your souls. For my yoke is easy and my burden is light."

(John 14:27 NIV) Peace I leave with you; my peace I give you. I do not give to you as the world gives. Do not let your hearts be troubled and do not be afraid.

(John 16:33 NIV) "I have told you these things, so that in me you may have peace. In this world you will have trouble. But take heart! I have overcome the world."

(Luke 7:5 NIV) because he loves our nation and has built our synagogue."

(Romans 14:17-19 NIV) For the kingdom of God is not a matter of eating and drinking, but of righteousness, peace and joy in the Holy Spirit, because anyone who serves Christ in this way is pleasing to God and approved by men. Let us therefore make every effort to do what leads to peace and to mutual edification.
(1 Corinthians 14:33 NIV) For God is not a God of disorder but of peace. As in all the congregations of the saints,

(2 Thessalonians 3:16 NIV) Now may the Lord of peace himself give you peace at all times and in every way. The Lord be with all of you.
(Romans 15:13 NIV) May the God of hope fill you with all joy and peace as you trust in him, so that you may overflow with hope by the power of the Holy Spirit.

Deliverance

Psalm 34:4, 7 — I sought the LORD, and he answered me; he delivered me from all my fears. 7 The angel
of the LORD encamps around those who fear him, and he delivers them. (NIV)

Life can feel like you're on a slippery slope most of the time. There are many times in life when we find ourselves in situations that are way over our heads, whether it is taking on a house note or car payment that is over our budget or getting ourselves caught in an addiction with drugs, alcohol, or sexual sin. There are also times when life brings trouble your way and you had nothing to do with it. Car accidents, hostage holdups, or being caught in a natural disaster can occur at any time, and it can leave us in a helpless place. God promises us in His Word that He is an ever present help in the time of trouble (Psalm 46:1). God is willing and able to deliver us from any type of problem we find ourselves in, even if we are to blame for the problem.

David, in the 34th book of Psalms, gives God praise because the Lord stayed faithful in His deliverance of David from the hands of Abimelek. David makes a statement in Psalm 34:4 that we need to make every day in our lives. He says, *"I sought the LORD and he answered me."* We can have faith in the fact that when we find ourselves in life's storms and things seem out of control, God will answer our cry for help. No matter what the addiction is or how deep we may be in debt, God will hear us and deliver us out of the circumstance.

David is a prime example of God's deliverance power; he was delivered from the wrath of Saul, Goliath, a lion, and a bear just to name a few. Throughout the books of Psalms we find David constantly praying for God to deliver him from something or someone. David was a man who put his total trust in God and did not rely on his own abilities. David was a great king who had a lot of wealth. But he wisely knew that having God on his side was more than the whole

world against him (Romans 8:31).

Psalm 34:7 tells us that the angel of the Lord encamps around those who fear Him.

When you look up the word *encamp,* you will find that it means *to settle or to lodge in.* This is an

exciting verse for believers, because God reveals that His deliverance plan is already in place for

us before we get into trouble. His angel is waiting and ready to bring us out of any problem we

find ourselves in. The second part of verse seven reveals this to us. It says, *"and he delivers them."*

Our God is a proactive God, and He will not just sit back and let us be crushed. He will come to

our rescue and deliver us from any danger or circumstance we may encounter in life. We need

to learn this through His Word and make it a statement of fact every day in our lives. There is

no problem too big for God! He promises us in His Word that He will deliver us if we ask Him

to.

As you study the scriptures on deliverance, remember to speak them over your life and

your family's life every day. Lock your faith in God; it doesn't matter what you may be going

through or how long you have been going through it. Remember that you have a right to be

delivered as a believer, and all you have to do is ask God like David did and watch God come

to the rescue.

What areas in your life do you need God's deliverance in? Have you asked God for help,

or have you been trying to solve your problems on your own?

Deliverance Scriptures

(Genesis 45:7 NIV) But God sent me ahead of you to preserve for you a remnant on earth and to save your lives by a great deliverance.

(Exodus 14:13 NIV) Moses answered the people, "Do not be afraid. Stand firm and you will see the deliverance the LORD will bring you today. The Egyptians you see today you will never see again.

(Joshua 6:2 NIV) Then the LORD said to Joshua, "See, I have delivered Jericho into your hands, along with its king and its fighting men.

(Judges 3:9 NIV) But when they cried out to the LORD, he raised up for them a deliverer, Othniel son of Kenaz, Caleb's younger brother, who saved them.

(1 Samuel 10:18 NIV) "This is what the LORD, the God of Israel, says: 'I brought Israel up out of Egypt, and I delivered you from the power of Egypt and all the kingdoms that oppressed you.

(1 Samuel 17:37 NIV) The LORD who delivered me from the paw of the lion and the paw of the bear will deliver me from the hand of this Philistine." Saul said to David, "Go, and the LORD be with you."

(2 Samuel 22:1-2 NIV) David sang to the LORD the words of this song when the LORD delivered him from the hand of all his enemies and from the hand of Saul. "The LORD is my rock, my fortress and my deliverer;

(2 Samuel 22:44 NIV) "You have delivered me from the attacks of my people; you have preserved me as the head of nations. People I did not know are subject to me,

(1 Kings 20:28 NIV) The man of God came up and told the king of Israel, "This is what the LORD says: 'Because the Arameans think the LORD is a god of the hills and not a god of the valleys, I will deliver this vast army into your hands, and you will know that I am the LORD."

(2 Kings 13:5 NIV) The LORD provided a deliverer for Israel, and they escaped from the power of Aram. So the Israelites lived in their own homes as they had before.

(2 Kings 17:39 NIV) Rather, worship the LORD your God; it is he who will deliver you from the hand of all your enemies."

(2 Chronicles 20:17 NIV) You will not have to fight this battle. Take up your positions; stand firm and see the deliverance the LORD will give you, O Judah and Jerusalem. Do not be afraid; do not be discouraged. Go out to face them tomorrow, and the LORD will be with you.

(Job 22:30 NIV) He will deliver even one who is not innocent, who will be delivered through the cleanness of your hands."

(Psalm 3:8 NIV) From the LORD comes deliverance. May your blessing be on your people.

(Psalm 18:2 NIV) The LORD is my rock, my fortress and my deliverer; my God is my rock, in whom I take refuge. He is my shield and the horn of my salvation, my stronghold.

(Psalm 32:7 NIV) You are my hiding place; you will protect me from trouble and surround me with songs of deliverance.

(Psalm 33:18, 19 NIV) But the eyes of the LORD are on those who fear him, on those whose hope is in his unfailing love, to deliver them from death and keep them alive in famine

(Psalm 34:4 NIV) I sought the LORD, and he answered me; he delivered me from all my fears.

(Psalm 72:12 NIV) For he will deliver the needy who cry out, the afflicted who have no one to help.

(Psalm 86:13 NIV) For great is your love toward me; you have delivered me from the depths of the grave.

(Psalm 91:15 NIV) He will call upon me, and I will answer him; I will be with him in trouble, I will deliver him and honor him.

(Psalm 107:6 NIV) Then they cried out to the LORD in their trouble, and he delivered them from their distress.

(Psalm 140:7 NIV) O Sovereign LORD, my strong deliverer, who shields my head in the day of battle -

(Psalm 144:2 NIV) He is my loving God and my fortress, my stronghold and my deliverer, my shield, in whom I take refuge, who subdues peoples under me.

(Jeremiah 42:11 NIV) Do not be afraid of the king of Babylon, whom you now fear. Do not be afraid of him, declares the LORD, for I am with you and will save you and deliver you from his hands.

(Joel 2:32 NIV) And everyone who calls on the name of the LORD will be saved; for on Mount Zion and in Jerusalem there will be deliverance, as the LORD has said, among the survivors whom the LORD calls.

(2 Corinthians 1:10 NIV) He has delivered us from such a deadly peril, and he will deliver us. On him we have set our hope that he will continue to deliver us,

(2 Timothy 4:17 NIV) But the Lord stood at my side and gave me strength, so that through me the message might be fully proclaimed and all the Gentiles might hear it. And I was delivered from the lion's mouth.

(Psalm 6:4 NIV) Turn, O LORD, and deliver me; save me because of your unfailing love.

(Psalm 31:1 NIV) In you, O LORD, I have taken refuge; let me never be put to shame; deliver me in your righteousness.

(Psalm 31:15 NIV) My times are in your hands; deliver me from my enemies and from those who pursue me.

(Psalm 40:17 NIV) Yet I am poor and needy; may the Lord think of me. You are my help and my deliverer; O my God, do not delay.

(Psalm 119:117 NIV) Uphold me, and I will be delivered; I will always have regard for your decrees.

(Psalm 119:153 NIV) Look upon my suffering and deliver me, for I have not forgotten your law.

(Psalm 119:170 NIV) May my supplication come before you; deliver me according to your promise.

(Psalm 144:7 NIV) Reach down your hand from on high; deliver me and rescue me from the mighty waters, from the hands of foreigners

(Psalm 144:11 NIV) Deliver me and rescue me from the hands of foreigners whose mouths are full of lies, whose right hands are deceitful.

(Matthew 6:13 NIV) And lead us not into temptation, but deliver us from the evil one.

Prosperity

Joshua 1:7-8 – "Be strong and very courageous. Be careful to obey all the law my servant Moses gave you; do not turn from it to the right or to the left, that you may be successful wherever you go. Keep this Book of the Law always on your lips; meditate on it day and night, so that you may be careful to do everything written in it. Then you will be prosperous and successful. (NIV)

Prosperity is a topic we hear about every week at most churches and that we see every day when we turn on the TV from our news media. Stock tickers are found throughout the Internet, keeping us abreast of what is going on with the world's economies. If you stay up late at night, you will find countless infomercials of "wealth gurus" telling you how you can make a millions dollars if you buy their program. All around us is this drive to acquire wealth and to live with more than enough. It is because of this passion that many people steal, kill, lie, and ruin other peoples' lives in the hunt to become prosperous.

God never intended for people to act like crabs in a bucket, doing everything we can to achieve wealth even at the cost of other people or our natural environment. God designed the earth knowing how many people would eventually live on it and how much everyone would need to survive. But many have taken their trust away from God's plan for provision and decided to try to take care of themselves. As believers, we must remember that God desires for us to be prosperous and to live with security that all of our needs will be met.

In Joshua 1:7-8, God gives us a clear understanding of how we can live in prosperity in our lives. He also essentially shows us that He desires for us to be prosperous, but it takes cooperation on our part. I believe it is important for us to understand that not only does God want us to live in prosperity, but it is equally important to Him *how* He wants prosperity to manifest itself in our lives.

In Joshua chapter one, the position of power is being transferred from Moses to Joshua, who would then take the leadership role over the children of Israel. God was speaking with Joshua, and He was giving him a secret to success in life. He tells him first to be "*strong and courageous.*" To achieve anything in life, you cannot let fear rule over you. You will have to stand strong and act courageously in the thing that you want to have success in. Then He told Joshua not to forget the Law of Moses. The Law of Moses was God's Word and the rules Moses had put in place for the children of Israel to live by. God told Joshua that his focus needed to stay on His Word in order for him to have success (Joshua 1:7).

This is an extremely important concept to let sink into our minds and spirits. God told Joshua that in order for him to be prosperous, he had to follow his Word. I believe God reveals a new concept of what prosperity is to us here. Prosperity in today's society is viewed as *material wealth,* but God's prosperity is not limited to just money. God's prosperity will run over to every area of your life if you let it.

It will allow you to be a great leader on your job, just as Joshua became while leading the children of Israel. It will run over onto your physical body and cause you to be healed of sickness so you can live a healthy life. It will touch your children and their futures, and it will give you favor with a person that could put you in a position where you can have more money than you ever dreamed was possible. God goes on to reiterate this point in verse eight; He tells Joshua to keep His Word on his lips and to meditate on His Word daily.

This is the key to success for our lives as believers—to keep speaking what God speaks and to keep His Word as our ruling thoughts. When we live in this manner, God says that "*then you will be prosperous and successful*" (Joshua 1:8). Many people try to be prosperous without God, and yes, they may obtain a lot of money, but they may lose their families in the process. They may make millions or billions of dollars a year, but they are so stressed that their health doesn't permit them to enjoy the money. We as Kingdom Citizens cannot live by the standard of prosperity that is in the world, which is solely the accumulation of money. We have the right to be prosperous by God's standards, and it is not limited to just money.

God desires for us to have material wealth, but His desires are not limited to that. Let us follow the key to success God gave Joshua, which was to keep His Word as the guide for our lives. Let us follow God's example of how we should give, communicate with our environment, talk, act, deal with others, and view life overall, and we can be assured if we do this we will live in prosperity and have good success (Joshua 1:8). Remember to study these verses on God's promises to you. Meditate on them and speak them over your life and family every day, and have faith that God will begin to fulfill His Word for you, and then watch it happen.

What areas in your life are you not seeing God's prosperity? What have you defined as prosperity, and does it line up with God's Word?

Prosperity Scriptures

(Deuteronomy 8:18 NIV) But remember the LORD your God, for it is he who gives you the ability to produce wealth, and so confirms his covenant, which he swore to your ancestors, as it is today.

(Joshua 1:7,8 NIV) "Be strong and very courageous. Be careful to obey all the law my servant Moses gave you; do not turn from it to the right or to the left, that you may be successful wherever you go. Keep this Book of the Law always on your lips; meditate on it day and night, so that you may be careful to do everything written in it. Then you will be prosperous and successful.

(Genesis 12:1-3 NIV) The LORD had said to Abram, "Go from your country, your people and your father's household to the land I will show you. I will make you into a great nation, and I will bless you; I will make your name great, and you will be a blessing. I will bless those who bless you, and whoever curses you I will curse; and all peoples on earth will be blessed through you..

(Psalm 1:1-3 NIV) Blessed is the one who does not walk in step with the wicked or stand in the way that sinners take or sit in the company of mockers,² but whose delight is in the law of the LORD, and who meditates on his law day and night. ³ That person is like a tree planted by streams of water, which yields its fruit in season and whose leaf does not wither- whatever they do prospers..

(1 Chronicles 4:10 NIV) Jabez cried out to the God of Israel, "Oh, that you would bless me and enlarge my territory! Let your hand be with me, and keep me from harm so that I will be free from pain." And God granted his request.

(Psalm 35:27 KJV) Let them shout for joy, and be glad, that favour my righteous cause:, let them say continually, Let the Lord be magnified, which hath pleasure in the prosperity of his servant.

(Psalm 34:8-11 NIV) Taste and see that the LORD is good; blessed is the one who takes refuge in him. ⁹ Fear the LORD, you his holy people, for those who fear him lack nothing. ¹⁰ The lions may grow weak and hungry, but those who seek the LORD lack no good thing. ¹¹ Come, my children, listen to me; I will teach you the fear of the LORD.

(Psalm 84:11 NIV) For the LORD God is a sun and shield; the LORD bestows favor and honor; no good thing does he withhold from those whose walk is blameless..

(Psalm 37:22-26 NIV) those the LORD blesses will inherit the land, but those he curses will be destroyed. ²³ The LORD makes firm the steps of the one who delights in him; ²⁴ though he may stumble, he will not fall, for the LORD upholds him with his hand. ²⁵ I was young and now I am old, yet I have never seen the righteous forsaken or their children begging bread. ²⁶ They are always generous and lend freely; their children will be a blessing.

(Psalm 55:22 NIV) Cast your cares on the LORD and he will sustain you; he will never let the righteous be shaken..

(Psalm 71:21 KJV) Thou shalt increase my greatness, and comfort me on every side.

(Proverbs 3:9-10 NIV) Honor the LORD with your wealth, with the firstfruits of all your crops; [10] then your barns will be filled to overflowing, and your vats will brim over with new wine..

(Proverbs 8:18-21 NIV) With me are riches and honor, enduring wealth and prosperity. [19] My fruit is better than fine gold; what I yield surpasses choice silver. [20] I walk in the way of righteousness, along the paths of justice, [21] bestowing a rich inheritance on those who love me and making their treasuries full.

(Proverbs 10:4 NIV) Lazy hands make for poverty, but diligent hands bring wealth.

(Proverbs 13:22 NIV) A good person leaves an inheritance for their children's children, but a sinner's wealth is stored up for the righteous..

(Proverbs 22:9 NIV) The generous will themselves be blessed, for they share their food with the poor.

(Proverbs 22:29 NIV) Do you see someone skilled in their work? They will serve before kings; they will not serve before officials of low rank.

(Malachi 3:10-12 NIV) Bring the whole tithe into the storehouse, that there may be food in my house. Test me in this," says the LORD Almighty, "and see if I will not throw open the floodgates of heaven and pour out so much blessing that there will not be room enough to store it. [11] I will prevent pests from devouringyour crops, and the vines in your fields will not drop their fruit before it is ripe," says the LORDAlmighty. [12] "Then all the nations will call you blessed, for yours will be a delightful land," says the LORD Almighty.

(Matthew 6:25-34 NIV) "Therefore I tell you, do not worry about your life, what you will eat or drink; or about your body, what you will wear. Is not life more than food, and the body more than clothes? [26] Look at the birds of the air; they do not sow or reap or store away in barns, and yet your heavenly Father feeds them. Are you not much more valuable than they? [27] Can any one of you by worrying add a single hour to your life[.]?

[28] "And why do you worry about clothes? See how the flowers of the field grow. They do not labor or spin. [29] Yet I tell you that not even Solomon in all his splendor was dressed like one of these. [30] If that is how God clothes the grass of the field, which is here today and tomorrow is thrown into the fire, will he not much more clothe you — you of little faith? [31] So do not worry, saying, 'What shall we eat?' or 'What shall we drink?' or 'What shall we wear?' [32] For the pagans run after all these things, and your heavenly Father knows that you need them. [33] But seek first his kingdom and his righteousness, and all these things will be given to you as well. [34] Therefore do not worry about tomorrow, for tomorrow will worry about itself. Each day has enough trouble of its own.

(Matthew 7:7-11NIV) Ask and it will be given to you; seek and you will find; knock and the door will be opened to you.[8] For everyone who asks receives; the one who seeks finds; and to the one who knocks, the door will be opened. [9] "Which of you, if your son asks for bread, will give him a stone? [10] Or if he asks for a fish, will give him a snake? [11] If you, then, though you are evil, know how to give good gifts to your children, how much more will your Father in heaven give good gifts to those who ask him!.

(Luke 6:38 NIV) Give, and it will be given to you. A good measure, pressed down, shaken together and running over, will be poured into your lap. For with the measure you use, it will be measured to you."

(John 14:14 NIV) You may ask me for anything in my name, and I will do it.

(2 Corinthians 8:9 NIV) For you know the grace of our Lord Jesus Christ, that though he was rich, yet for your sake he became poor, so that you through his poverty might become rich.

(Philippians 4:19 NIV) And my God will meet all your needs according to the riches of his glory in Christ Jesus.

(1 Timothy 6:17 NIV) Command those who are rich in this present world not to be arrogant nor to put their hope in wealth, which is so uncertain, but to put their hope in God, who richly provides us with everything for our enjoyment.

(1 John 4:4 NIV) You, dear children, are from God and have overcome them, because the one who is in you is greater than the one who is in the world.

(3 John 1:2 KJV) Beloved, I wish above all things that thou mayest prosper and be in health, even as thy soul prospereth.

Protection

Psalm 4:8 — In peace I will lie down and sleep, for you alone, LORD, make me dwell in safety. (NIV)

Security is a top priority in any person's life. People want to feel safe and secure as they go about their daily lives. Here in the U.S., military spending is always a hot topic because we want to make sure as a nation that we have a strong military so that we can protect ourselves from enemies. Millions of dollars are spent each year, my Americans, on firearms and other safety precautions, because people are willing to do whatever it takes to protect themselves. As believers, our trust for protection is not in our country's military or in the firearm we may personally own. Our protection comes from the Lord. The Bible clearly teaches us in that God is our refuge and a very present help in the time of trouble (Psalm 46:1).

In Psalm 4:8, David gives us a great example of how we are to respond to the fact that God is our protector. David says, *"I will lie down and sleep."* Not many people can sleep in the times of war unless you have total faith in your fellow soldiers to protect your camp while you rest. David was a king who fought in many battles and had many enemies, but he still could get some sleep. Why? Because God promised David through His Word that He would protect and keep David.

God promises us throughout the whole Bible that He will be there to protect and comfort us in all situations. There is nothing that God fears or has not seen. God created EVERYTHING! As believers, you have the person who created the earth and everything in it on your side, so when people or situations come into your life, you can rest assured that the *created thing* will not defeat the *creator*! In 2 Chronicles 32, Sennacherib, the king of Assyria, was threatening to rage war against Hezekiah and Jerusalem. Hezekiah, in verses 7 and 8, had to encourage the people that the army that stood against them could not compare to the power they had on their side. And he reminds Jerusalem that the Assyrians only fought with the "*arm of the flesh*," which meant they were only as strong as their skill level allowed them to be. But they fought with the "*LORD our God*" on their side. It was the God of heaven and earth fighting not just with them but for them. Hezekiah's message to Jerusalem back then is the same message we need to remember today; we have all the power of heaven and earth fighting on our side, so who or what can stand against us! Let us make sure we put our trust for protection in the Lord at all times, even if we have our own guns or we live in a country that has a strong military, which is great. But as believers, we know that God watches over us, and it is He who promises to protect us. God's protection comes in many different ways, so let us remain prayerful on how God desires to protect each one of us.

As you study the Bible verses pertaining to your God-given right to be protected by the best heaven has to offer, remember to speak God's protection over your life and your family every day. Pray to God for His protection in every area of your life, and meditate on His Word so that you can weed out any thoughts of fear when life gets tough.

Do you ask God for His protection over every area of your life, or do you pick and choose what you want Him to protect? What areas haven't you surrendered to God's protection that you try to rely on your own means to protect? Do you ask God to protect something but still fear for its safety?

Protection Scriptures

(Proverbs 18:10 NIV) - The name of the Lord is a strong tower; the righteous run to it and are safe.

(Psalm 121:2-3 NIV) My help comes from the Lord, the Maker of heaven and earth. He will not let your foot slip--he who watches over you will not slumber.

(Psalm 121:7-8 NIV) - The Lord will keep you from all harm--he will watch over your life; The Lord will watch over your coming and going both now and for evermore.

(Psalm 27:1 NIV) The LORD is my light and my salvation—whom shall I fear? The LORD is the stronghold of my life— of whom shall I be afraid?

(Psalm 4:8 NIV) In peace I will lie down and sleep, for you alone, LORD, make me dwell in safety.

(Psalm 91:9-11 NIV) If you say, "The LORD is my refuge, "and you make the Most High your dwelling, [10] no harm will overtake you, no disaster will come near your tent. [11] For he will command his angels concerning you to guard you in all your ways;

(Matthew 16:18 NIV) And I tell you that you are Peter, and on this rock I will build my church, and the gates of Hades will not overcome it.

(2Thessalonians 3:3 NIV) But the Lord is faithful, and he will strengthen you and protect you from the evil one.

(1Peter 2:9 NIV) But you are a chosen people, a royal priesthood, a holy nation, God's special possession, that you may declare the praises of him who called you out of darkness into his wonderful light.

(Hebrews 13:5 NIV) Keep your lives free from the love of money and be content with what you have, because God has said, "Never will I leave you; never will I forsake you.

(Isaiah 54:17 NIV) no weapon forged against you will prevail, and you will refute every tongue that accuses you. This is the heritage of the servants of the LORD, and this is their vindication from me," declares the LORD.

(2Timothy 4:18 NIV) The Lord will rescue me from every evil attack and will bring me safely to his heavenly kingdom. To him be glory for ever and ever. Amen.

Guidance

Proverbs 3:5-6 — Trust in the LORD with all your heart and lean not on your own understanding; [6] in all

your ways submit to him, and he will make your paths straight. (NIV)

Clear direction on how to navigate through life can be hard to find most of the time. Life is filled with so many twists and turns that it leaves people running in circles not able to find their way. Corporations pay their executives top dollar to guide the company in the right direction. Sports teams seek coaches that can properly utilize the talent on the team and guide the team to a championship. Good leaders that have the ability to take someone or something from one level to the next are a sought after commodity in our day and age. Every nation in the world looks for good leaders to guide the nation into prosperity. We have had some great leaders in our day and age, from Dr. Martin Luther King Jr., Nelson Mandela, Steve Jobs, Warren Buffet, and Dr. Jerry Buss. These individuals were able to guide their businesses, sports teams, political movements, and country to unbelievable success. Their visions have shaped our world today.

But with all of their achievements and accolades, it does not compare to God guiding a person's life. These individuals have had great ideas that have changed the course of how we view life or business, but they are still just men and limited in their knowledge. If we can look at the world today and see the impact they had on it and even the personal impact of what they have done in our lives. What do you think God can do for you if you allow Him to guide your life? If man can leave an impact on you, what can God leave if we surrender to Him?

Proverbs 3:5-6 is a promise from the Lord. God tells us that if we don't trust in our own intellect, skills, resources, connections, or good looks, He will guide us through life. We have had some great visionaries in our time; they can only have *hope* of the future, but our God *knows* what the future holds! We need to put our trust in the one who holds the future. God has a plan for our lives, and these plans have our best interests in mind. God speaks to us in Jeremiah 29:11, and this is what He reveals to us, *"For I know the plans I have for you," declares the* LORD, *"plans to prosper you and not to harm you, plans to give you hope and a future"* (NIV).

God tells us what He desires for our futures, and it sounds wonderful! God tells us He has preset plans. This should give us the confidence to surrender the direction of our lives over to Him. God has already plotted out the best course and is waiting for us to start walking it.

This is an amazing benefit for us as believers, because we don't have to worry about all the uncertainties of life; God has worked out all the problems in our favor prior to our journey. All we have to do is let Him guide us and reap the benefits. The latter part of Jeremiah 29:11 shows us this fact. God says to us that the plans He has for us are designed to lead us to prosperity; they won't hurt us, and they will give us hope of a bright future! This is what every nation in the world is trying to accomplish for its citizens, and God reveals this is what He has in store for us.

Here in the U.S., our country has done a great job of giving its citizens the best opportunities to achieve financial success, societal stability, and an overall good quality of life. But with all of its success, it still falls way short of its goal. God, on the other hand, has never failed, He has never missed a deadline, and He has never fallen short of a goal either. If we can trust our nation's leaders to give us a hope for the future, then we have to give God a try if we have not already. Man has good intentions, but God gets things done!

As part of our inheritance as Kingdom Citizens, we have the right to have God guide our lives each day. When we became born again, we actually became God's responsibility, because He is our King and we are His citizens; the welfare of citizens is the King's responsibility in a kingdom. Here in the U.S., you as an individual are responsible for your own welfare in a democracy. But as a citizen in God's kingdom, God is responsible for you because He is the King. So, let us allow Him to operate in our life as our king and guide us in the direction He has planned; this will lead us to hope, prosperity, and an awesome future.

Remember as you study the scriptures of God's promise to guide your life to not just read the verses to gain knowledge, but make sure you are applying them in your life daily. Let God guide you in your decision making in every area of your life; He promises if you do you will be happy you did. Speak the Word of God over your life, and meditate on it daily; then watch God reveal the benefits to you.

Have you totally surrendered to God guiding you in every area of life? What areas do you struggle to let God take control of? Do you fear letting go and letting God?

Guidance Scriptures

(Psalm 16:11 NIV) You make known to me the path of life; you will fill me with joy in your presence, with eternal pleasures at your right hand.

(Psalm 23:1 NIV) The Lord is my shepherd, I lack nothing.

(Psalm 32:8 NIV) I will instruct you and teach you in the way you should go; I will counsel you with my loving eye on you.

(Psalm 37:23 ESV) The steps of a man are established by the LORD, when he delights in his way;

(Psalm 119:105 NIV) Your word is a lamp to my feet and a light to my path.

(Proverbs 3:5-6 NIV) Trust in the LORD with all your heart and lean not on your own understanding; [6] in all your ways submit to him, and he will make your paths straight.

(Isaiah 30:21 NIV) Whether you turn to the right or to the left, your ears will hear a voice behind you, saying, "This is the way; walk in it."

(Isaiah 48:17 NIV) This is what the LORD says—your Redeemer, the Holy One of Israel: "I am the LORD your God, who teaches you what is best for you, who directs you in the way you should go.

(Isaiah 58:11 NIV) The LORD will guide you always; he will satisfy your needs in a sun-scorched land and will strengthen your frame. You will be like a well-watered garden, like a spring whose waters never fail.

(John 8:12 NIV) When Jesus spoke again to the people, he said, "I am the light of the world. Whoever follows me will never walk in darkness, but will have the light of life."

(John 10:3-5 NIV) The gatekeeper opens the gate for him, and the sheep listen to his voice. He calls his own sheep by name and leads them out. [4] When he has brought out all his own, he goes on ahead of them, and his sheep follow him because they know his voice. [5] But they will never follow a stranger; in fact, they will run away from him because they do not recognize a stranger's voice."

(John 16:13 NIV) But when he, the Spirit of truth, comes, he will guide you into all the truth. He will not speak on his own; he will speak only what he hears, and he will tell you what is yet to come.

(Romans 8:14 NIV) For those who are led by the Spirit of God are the children of God.

(Philippians 2:13 NIV) for it is God who works in you to will and to act in order to fulfill his good purpose.

(Colossians 3:15 NIV) Let the peace of Christ rule in your hearts, since as members of one body you were called to peace. And be thankful.

(Colossians 4:12 NIV) Epaphras, who is one of you and a servant of Christ Jesus, sends greetings. He is always wrestling in prayer for you, that you may stand firm in all the will of God, mature and fully assured

(Hebrews 13:21 NIV) equip you with everything good for doing his will, and may he work in us what is pleasing to him, through Jesus Christ, to whom be glory for ever and ever. Amen.

Attitude

Ephesians 4:1-3 — As a prisoner for the Lord, then, I urge you to live a life worthy of the calling you have

received.² Be completely humble and gentle; be patient, bearing with one another in love. ³ Make every

effort to keep the unity of the Spirit through the bond of peace. (NIV)

Attitude is considered by scholars, business executives, and leaders of countries as one

of the most important attributes a person must have in check to be successful at any level of

business or in life. A person's attitude can make or break their relationships with others or their

achievement in business. The Bible has many scriptures focusing on one's attitude, because as

believers, our attitudes are a part of our witness to others in regards to our faith. How we act

and react to life is on constant display to the world whether we want it to be or not. People are

watching us and how we respond to situations, and it is important that they see us have a

positive attitude daily.

Many people believe that their attitude towards others should be based on how that

person treats them. But this is not the philosophy that a believer should live by. Our attitude is

based on how good God is to us, not on how good man is to us. With this thought in mind, as a

believer we can/should have a good attitude **ALL** the time! Why? Because God is **ALWAYS**

good! Even when life gets frustrating and stressful, we know that we do not have to let the

circumstances affect our overall attitude. We have power by the Holy Spirit to turn our attitude

around immediately! This is one of the benefits of being a believer.

The apostle Paul continually encouraged the churches He wrote letters to, to be mindful

of their attitude. He always reminded them to show Christ in their lives, and one of the best

ways was having a great attitude towards life. In Ephesians 4:1-3, Paul is writing to the church at Ephesus from prison, urging them to remember the calling on their lives. And in doing so they must be watchful of how they act and respond to each other. He encouraged them to be *"humble and gentle"* (Ephesians 4:2). Humility is an attribute not found often in U.S. society, and when it is found in someone, they stand out amongst others. Being humble is important for us as believers, because it reflects Christ in our lives. Christ, the Bible says, humbled Himself for us (Philippians 2:8).

Paul also tells us here in Ephesians to be patient and loving to each other. When we have a Christ-like attitude, it will always lead us to being patient with people. We must understand that people are not perfect, and they will always fail you. Even our children, who we raised, will disappoint us. We could have taught them good values and morals, but they will inevitably still make mistakes. We are the same with God; we fall every day and come short of God's standards. But He never gives up on us, so we can't give up on people either.

We have to show the love of Christ daily, because people expect us to as believers. Even if they don't believe in our God, they still anticipate us living the principles of the Word of God. This is especially true in regards to our attitudes. And as believers, it is absolutely possible for us to live life with a Christ-like attitude. Even if we were raised in a family where negative attitudes were a norm, when we accepted Christ as our Lord and Savior **all** the old non Christ-like characteristics died with our sins. That included our bad attitudes! We now live as a new creation, and we have the right to live life with a positive attitude every day.

A good attitude is a result of a good thought life. What we think about is what we become (Proverbs 23:7). If we have positive thoughts, we will have a positive attitude towards life. But if we are constantly thinking about how bad our circumstances are or how life isn't fair or about how we don't have this or that, we are going to have a bad attitude.

Your thought life is the first step towards a Christ-like attitude, so it is important that you fill your mind with the Word of God. This will keep you with the right perspective on and response to life. The Bible tells us to keep our mind on things that are, true, noble, pure, admirable, excellent, or praiseworthy (Philippians 4:8). If we keep our thoughts on things that fall into these categories, we will find that our attitude is not hard to keep under control. A good attitude is not something that comes overnight; it takes time to truly develop, but as we study and meditate on God's Word every day, our attitudes will reflect Christ. Then our relationships with others and success in our businesses, with our children, and in our marriages will reap the benefits of it.

As you are studying God's Word on attitude, remember to speak God's Word over your life daily so that the Word gets into your thoughts, which will impact your attitude. You are in total control of your attitude, so make sure you don't let it control you.

Does your attitude towards life reflect Christ's? In what areas does your attitude need adjustments? Do you have a positive or negative thought life? Would God be pleased with your daily thoughts?

Attitude Scriptures

(1 Peter 3:13 NIV) Who is going to harm you if you are eager to do good?

(Matthew 6:33 NIV) But seek first his kingdom and his righteousness, and all these things will be given to you as well.

(Ephesians 4:2-5 NIV) Be completely humble and gentle; be patient, bearing with one another in love. [3] Make every effort to keep the unity of the Spirit through the bond of peace. [4] There is one body and one Spirit, just as you were called to one hope when you were called; [5] one Lord, one faith, one baptism;

(Ephesians 4:12-16 NIV) to equip his people for works of service, so that the body of Christ may be built up [13] until we all reach unity in the faith and in the knowledge of the Son of God and become mature, attaining to the whole measure of the fullness of Christ. [14] Then we will no longer be infants, tossed back and forth by the waves, and blown here and there by every wind of teaching and by the cunning and craftiness of people in their deceitful scheming. [15] Instead, speaking the truth in love, we will grow to become in every respect the mature body of him who is the head, that is, Christ. [16] From him the whole body, joined and held together by every supporting ligament, grows and builds itself up in love, as each part does its work.

(Ephesians 2:8-9 NIV) For it is by grace you have been saved, through faith—and this is not from yourselves, it is the gift of God— [9] not by works, so that no one can boast.

(Galatians 3:28 NIV) There is neither Jew nor Gentile, neither slave nor free, nor is there male and female, for you are all one in Christ Jesus.

(Isaiah 40:8 NIV) The grass withers and the flowers fall, but the word of our God endures forever."

(Romans 6:14 NIV) For sin shall no longer be your master, because you are not under the law, but under grace.

(Romans 3:28 NIV) For we maintain that a person is justified by faith apart from the works of the law.

(Proverbs 15:1 NIV) A gentle answer turns away wrath, but a harsh word stirs up anger.

(Proverbs 18:21 NIV) The tongue has the power of life and death, and those who love it will eat its fruit.

Thought Life

Philippians 4:8 – Finally, brothers, whatever is true, whatever is noble, whatever is right, whatever is pure, whatever is lovely, whatever is admirable – if anything is excellent or praiseworthy – think about such things. (NIV)

A believer's thought life is one of the most critical areas that has to be guarded and nourished daily. Most of life's struggle does not come from outside influences but the inner battle that happens daily. I heard a great pastor say, "If you lose the battle between your ears, you will lose the fight in life." His point was that if your thought life was not positive, you would never win in life. The Bible puts a lot of emphasis on the thought life, because it is so important to our success. With all that Jesus did for us on the cross, if our thought life is negative, we will not walk in the victory that He died for us to have. Yes, God wants us to have a successful life, but if we don't do our part of keeping our thoughts on the things the Word of God tells us to, we won't be able to enjoy all that God has for us.

Paul, in Philippians 4:8, is speaking to the church there about keeping the proper thought life. He gives us great insight on what should consume our thoughts daily. He says we should be thinking on things that are, true, noble, right, pure, lovely, admirable, excellent, and praiseworthy. This is an incredible list and gives us clear direction in regards to what we need to keep our thoughts on. With our American culture being the way it is, most of the news or events we hear about are negative, so it can be hard to keep our thought life in proper order. But the good news is that no matter how many evil, negative, hateful, jealous, and rude things that are thrown at us daily, our God promises to guard our minds if we let Him. We must keep our mind on God and the things of God! Our minds should be consumed with what God has called us to do here on earth while we are here.

Many people I have found have a hard time keeping their minds on the things of God, because they are not fulfilling their God given destiny. When you are not walking in your calling, it is very easy to get sidetracked with the wrong people and wrong habits, which will always lead to a wrong thought life. The best way to protect your thoughts is to stay in God's Word daily and to be consistent in prayer and fulfilling your God-given assignment here on earth. When you keep these three habits every day, you won't have time to think about foolish things. And when negative thoughts are presented to you, you will be able to bypass them because you know how to; your knowledge of the Word will help you to realize you don't have any time to waste.

In Proverbs 23:7, a great principle is revealed about the importance of the thought life. It says, "as a man thinks in his hearts, so is he." Many times you will see the word heart in Scripture, but it also means mind as it does here in this verse. The Word of God reveals to us that we ultimately become what we think about. If we look at our lives honestly, it will reveal to us where our thoughts have been for the last 5, 10, or 20 years. If you want to change your future, you must change your thoughts today! You cannot live beyond your thoughts, so it is important that as believers we think on the Word of God daily; God only desires a good future for us full of prosperity and hope (Jeremiah 29:11).

As you study the Word of God about your thought life, remember to speak the Word of God over your life and mind daily. You have to meditate on God's Word so that it can take root in your mind if you want to have a correct thought life.

Does your thought life reflect the ideal thought life presented in Philippians 4:8? What people, habits, and environments do you need to remove in order for you to have the thought life God desires for you?

Thought Life Scriptures

(Philippians 4:8 ESV) Finally, brothers, whatever is true, whatever is honorable, whatever is just, whatever is pure, whatever is lovely, whatever is commendable, if there is any excellence, if there is anything worthy of praise, think about these things.

(Proverbs 17:22 ESV) A joyful heart is good medicine, but a crushed spirit dries up the bones.

(Philippians 4:6 ESV) Do not be anxious about anything, but in everything by prayer and supplication with thanksgiving let your requests be made known to God.

(Philippians 4:13 ESV) I can do all things through him who strengthens me.

(Jeremiah 29:11 ESV) For I know the plans I have for you, declares the Lord, plans for welfare and not for evil, to give you a future and a hope.

(Romans 12:2 ESV) Do not be conformed to this world, but be transformed by the renewal of your mind, that by testing you may discern what is the will of God, what is good and acceptable and perfect.

(Matthew 15:11 ESV) It is not what goes into the mouth that defiles a person, but what comes out of the mouth; this defiles a person."

(Ephesians 4:31-32 ESV) Let all bitterness and wrath and anger and clamor and slander be put away from you, along with all malice. Be kind to one another, tenderhearted, forgiving one another, as God in Christ forgave you.

(Proverbs 15:1 ESV) A soft answer turns away wrath, but a harsh word stirs up anger.

(Hebrews 13:5 ESV) Keep your life free from love of money, and be content with what you have, for he has said, "I will never leave you nor forsake you."

(Hebrews 13:6 ESV) So we can confidently say, "The Lord is my helper; I will not fear; what can man do to me?"

(Proverbs 18:21 ESV) Death and life are in the power of the tongue, and those who love it will eat its fruits.

(John 14:27 ESV) Peace I leave with you; my peace I give to you. Not as the world gives do I give to you. Let not your hearts be troubled, neither let them be afraid.

(1 John 1:9 ESV) If we confess our sins, he is faithful and just to forgive us our sins and to cleanse us from all unrighteousness.

(1 Peter 3:9 ESV) Do not repay evil for evil or reviling for reviling, but on the contrary, bless, for to this you were called, that you may obtain a blessing.

(Philippians 3:13-14 ESV) Brothers, I do not consider that I have made it my own. But one thing I do: forgetting what lies behind and straining forward to what lies ahead, I press on toward the goal for the prize of the upward call of God in Christ Jesus.

(Hebrews 4:12 ESV) For the word of God is living and active, sharper than any two-edged sword, piercing to the division of soul and of spirit, of joints and of marrow, and discerning the thoughts and intentions of the heart.

(Romans 8:28-31 ESV) And we know that for those who love God all things work together for good, for those who are called according to his purpose. For those whom he foreknew he also predestined to be conformed to the image of his Son, in order that he might be the firstborn among many brothers. And those whom he predestined he also called, and those whom he called he also justified, and those whom he justified he also glorified. What then shall we say to these things? If God is for us, who can be against us?

(Romans 10:13 ESV) For "everyone who calls on the name of the Lord will be saved."

(Proverbs 18:7 ESV) A fool's mouth is his ruin, and his lips are a snare to his soul.

(2 Corinthians 4:17-18 ESV) For this light momentary affliction is preparing for us an eternal weight of glory beyond all comparison, as we look not to the things that are seen but to the things that are unseen. For the things that are seen are transient, but the things that are unseen are eternal.

(1 John 4:4 ESV) Little children, you are from God and have overcome them, for he who is in you is greater than he who is in the world.

(Proverbs 24:10 ESV) If you faint in the day of adversity, your strength is small.

(1 John 4:1 ESV) Beloved, do not believe every spirit, but test the spirits to see whether they are from God, for many false prophets have gone out into the world.

(John 3:16 ESV) "For God so loved the world, that he gave his only Son, that whoever believes in him should not perish but have eternal life.

(Mark 11:22-25 ESV) And Jesus answered them, "Have faith in God. Truly, I say to you, whoever says to this mountain, 'Be taken up and thrown into the sea,' and does not doubt in his heart, but believes that what he says will come to pass, it will be done for him. Therefore I tell you, whatever you ask in prayer, believe that you have received it, and it will be yours. And whenever you stand praying, forgive, if you have anything against anyone, so that your Father also who is in heaven may forgive you your trespasses."

(Ephesians 4:23 ESV) And to be renewed in the spirit of your minds,

(Matthew 11:28-30 ESV) Come to me, all who labor and are heavy laden, and I will give you rest. Take my yoke upon you, and learn from me, for I am gentle and lowly in heart, and you will find rest for your souls. For my yoke is easy, and my burden is light."

(Proverbs 4:23 ESV) Keep your heart with all vigilance, for from it flow the springs of life.

(Philippians 2:5 ESV) Have this mind among yourselves, which is yours in Christ Jesus,

(Proverbs 15:2 ESV) The tongue of the wise commends knowledge, but the mouths of fools pour out folly.

(Psalm 118:24 ESV) This is the day that the Lord has made; let us rejoice and be glad in it.

(Psalm 50:15 ESV) And call upon me in the day of trouble; I will deliver you, and you shall glorify me."

(Romans 12:12 ESV) Rejoice in hope, be patient in tribulation, be constant in prayer.

(Nahum 1:7 ESV) The Lord is good, a stronghold in the day of trouble; he knows those who take refuge in him.

(Psalm 19:14 ESV) Let the words of my mouth and the meditation of my heart be acceptable in your sight, O Lord, my rock and my redeemer..

(Jeremiah 17:10 ESV) "I the Lord search the heart and test the mind, to give every man according to his ways, according to the fruit of his deeds."

(Psalm 34:8 ESV) Oh, taste and see that the Lord is good! Blessed is the man who takes refuge in him!

(Psalm 34:1 ESV) Of David, when he changed his behavior before Abimelech, so that he drove him out, and he went away. I will bless the Lord at all times; his praise shall continually be in my mouth.

(1 Thessalonians 5:16 ESV) Rejoice always,

(Psalm 1:2-3 ESV) But his delight is in the law of the Lord, and on his law he meditates day and night. He is like a tree planted by streams of water that yields its fruit in its season, and its leaf does not wither. In all that he does, he prospers.

Life of Purpose

Proverbs 19:21 — Many are the plans in a person's heart, but it is the LORD's purpose that prevails.

(NIV)

Many people ask the question, "What is my purpose for living?" Life can be demanding and even feel unmanageable at times. And if a person does not have a sense of their purpose for living, the pressures of life can cause a lot of stress, worry, frustration, and sickness. It is said that a person living life without a sense of their purpose is like the "walking dead." They move through life based on their feelings, and they end up following what everyone else does, because they do not know what they should be doing. One of the benefits of being a believer is that our God is a God of purpose; everything that He created He created with a purpose to fulfill. Every single person on earth has a purpose God designed them for. But without a relationship with God, man cannot find his true purpose, because it is linked with his Creator. As believers, we have already taken the first step in fulfilling our purpose on the earth, and we can rest assured in God that He will reveal to us His plans for us and the *how* to accomplish them!

Proverbs 19:21 says, *"Many are the plans in a person's heart, but it is the LORD's purpose that prevails."* Solomon, the writer of Proverbs, was the wisest man to ever live on the earth, and he reveals a key for living here. He says that man has many plans for his life, but God's purpose will prevail. As believers, we can be encouraged that our God is in control of everything! Our God is a God of purpose, and His purpose always comes to pass. So, with this knowledge, we know that if we put our trust in His guidance and direction, we will fulfill our purpose for life! God desires to reveal His purpose to us so that we have a full understanding of what it is we are assigned to do here on earth. We do not have to walk around stressed out because we don't

know "why we are here."

If we do not have a clear vision of our purpose yet, all we have to do is pray to God and

ask Him to show us what it is. He promises us in His Word that if we seek Him with our whole

heart, we will find Him (Jeremiah 29:13). As we seek God, we will ALWAYS find our purpose

or more clarity of it if we do have some knowledge already. As believers, we also know that the

plan God has for us is that we prosper in every area of life and that we have good success

(Jeremiah 29:11). God's purpose and plans for us will always lead us to the life we wanted in

the first place. Many times God's desires for us supersede even what we expected for ourselves.

We can have confidence that we do not have to live a purposeless life and that God will be there

to empower us every step of the way. He will never let life's temptations and attacks of Satan

overpower us. We will live a life of purpose!

As you study the scriptures on living a life of purpose, remember to speak the Word of

God over your life every day. Take time to meditate of God's Word, and in prayer, ask God to

continue to reveal to you His will for your life so that you can fulfill your assignment on earth.

What is your purpose for life? Have you asked God to reveal your purpose to you? Are

you trying to fulfill your own purpose for life or God's?

Life Purpose Scriptures

(Jeremiah 29:11 ESV) For I know the plans I have for you, declares the Lord, plans for welfare
and not for evil, to give you a future and a hope.

(Acts 26:16 ESV) But rise and stand upon your feet, for I have appeared to you for this purpose, to appoint you as a servant and witness to the things in which you have seen me and to those in which I will appear to you,

(Romans 8:28 ESV) And we know that for those who love God all things work together for good, for those who are called according to his purpose.

(Proverbs 16:9 ESV) The heart of man plans his way, but the Lord establishes his steps.

(Ephesians 1:11 ESV) In him we have obtained an inheritance, having been predestined according to the purpose of him who works all things according to the counsel of his will,

(Matthew 28:19 ESV) Go therefore and make disciples of all nations, baptizing them in the name of the Father and of the Son and of the Holy Spirit,

(1 Corinthians 6:19-20 ESV) Or do you not know that your body is a temple of the Holy Spirit within you, whom you have from God? You are not your own, for you were bought with a price. So glorify God in your body.

(John 15:16 ESV) You did not choose me, but I chose you and appointed you that you should go and bear fruit and that your fruit should abide, so that whatever you ask the Father in my name, he may give it to you.

(Ecclesiastes 12:13 ESV) The end of the matter; all has been heard. Fear God and keep his commandments, for this is the whole duty of man.

(Isaiah 14:27 ESV) For the Lord of hosts has purposed, and who will annul it? His hand is stretched out, and who will turn it back?

(Genesis 1:28 ESV) And God blessed them. And God said to them, "Be fruitful and multiply and fill the earth and subdue it and have dominion over the fish of the sea and over the birds of the heavens and over every living thing that moves on the earth."

(Ephesians 2:8-9 ESV) For by grace you have been saved through faith. And this is not your own doing; it is the gift of God, not a result of works, so that no one may boast.

(Isaiah 43:7 ESV) Everyone who is called by my name, whom I created for my glory, whom I formed and made."

(Isaiah 14:24 ESV) The Lord of hosts has sworn: "As I have planned, so shall it be, and as I have purposed, so shall it stand,

(1 John 2:3-4 ESV) And by this we know that we have come to know him, if we keep his commandments. Whoever says "I know him" but does not keep his commandments is a liar, and the truth is not in him,

(John 3:16 ESV) "For God so loved the world, that he gave his only Son, that whoever believes in him should not perish but have eternal life.

(Isaiah 14:26 ESV) This is the purpose that is purposed concerning the whole earth, and this is the hand that is stretched out over all the nations.

(Acts 22:16 ESV) And now why do you wait? Rise and be baptized and wash away your sins, calling on his name.'

(Philippians 3:9-10 ESV) And be found in him, not having a righteousness of my own that comes from the law, but that which comes through faith in Christ, the righteousness from God that depends on faith— that I may know him and the power of his resurrection, and may share his sufferings, becoming like him in his death,.

(1 Corinthians 6:12 ESV) "All things are lawful for me," but not all things are helpful. "All things are lawful for me," but I will not be enslaved by anything.

(Acts 2:38 ESV) And Peter said to them, "Repent and be baptized every one of you in the name of Jesus Christ for the forgiveness of your sins, and you will receive the gift of the Holy Spirit.

(Genesis 1:26-28 ESV) Then God said, "Let us make man in our image, after our likeness. And let them have dominion over the fish of the sea and over the birds of the heavens and over the livestock and over all the earth and over every creeping thing that creeps on the earth." So God created man in his own image, in the image of God he created him; male and female he created them. And God blessed them. And God said to them, "Be fruitful and multiply and fill the earth and subdue it and have dominion over the fish of the sea and over the birds of the heavens and over every living thing that moves on the earth."

(Jeremiah 1:5 ESV) "Before I formed you in the womb I knew you, and before you were born I consecrated you; I appointed you a prophet to the nations."

(Proverbs 15:22 ESV) Without counsel plans fail, but with many advisers they succeed.

(Isaiah 44:2 ESV) Thus says the Lord who made you, who formed you from the womb and will help you: Fear not, O Jacob my servant, Jeshurun whom I have chosen.

(Psalm 139:13-16 ESV) For you formed my inward parts; you knitted me together in my mother's womb. I praise you, for I am fearfully and wonderfully made. Wonderful are your works; my soul knows it very well. My frame was not hidden from you, when I was being made in secret, intricately woven in the depths of the earth. Your eyes saw my unformed substance; in your book were written, every one of them, the days that were formed for me, when as yet there was none of them.

(Mark 11:25 ESV) And whenever you stand praying, forgive, if you have anything against anyone, so that your Father also who is in heaven may forgive you your trespasses."

Prayer

John 14:13-14 – And I will do whatever you ask in my name, so that the Father may be glorified in the

Son. [14] You may ask me for anything in my name, and I will do it. (NIV)

Prayer is one of the greatest gifts we have as believers. Prayer gives us direct access to our Heavenly Father. We have this access because of the work Jesus Christ finished on Calvary's cross. When Christ was crucified and raised from the dead on the third day with all power in His hands, our relationship with our Heavenly Father was renewed. He paid the price for all of our sins so that we could have heavenly access again. Because of Jesus, we can stand boldly before God and ask Him for anything that is according to His will. We must understand that prayer is *not* simply just talking to God nor is it begging God for things. Prayer is lining ourselves up with God's desires, not our own. It is summiting to God's plans and listening for His direction for life.

The key to prayer is understanding that when you pray it is not just an opportunity for you to talk to God about yourself, but instead, we are to be intercessors for the world. Jesus is our greatest example for life, and He taught us how to have success in prayer in Matthew 6:9-13: *"This, then, is how you should pray: 'Our Father in heaven, hallowed be your name, your kingdom come, your will be done, on earth as it is in heaven. Give us today our daily bread. And forgive us our debts, as we also have forgiven our debtors. And lead us not into temptation, but deliver us from the evil one."*

Did you notice that Jesus shows us that we are start our prayer with praise (Our Father in heaven) to our Heavenly Father? This shows God that we acknowledge who He is in our lives, which is our Father. The word Father found here is *Abba* in the Greek, and it means "source and sustainer." So, literally, Jesus teaches us here that when we go before God in prayer, the first thing we need to do is acknowledge God as our *source* from which we depend on everything we need for life. Then we acknowledge Him as our *sustainer*. We put our trust in God to sustain us in every problem and trial that life throws our way.

Next Jesus says that we should ask that His Kingdom come and that His will be done on earth as it is in heaven. Here we are supposed to submit our lives to God's plans and purpose. In heaven, everything is as God says it is, and earth is supposed to be the same, but it requires us to allow God's will to be done. The reason for this is because God gave us all free will, and He will not force Himself on us; we have to agree to it. If you study the life of Jesus, He never forced Himself on people; when He sent out the 72 disciples, He told them that if people did not accept them, to brush the dust off their feet and keep on moving (Matthew 10:14). Here Jesus shows us the importance of praying for God's will to be done on the entire earth, not just in our lives.

Thirdly, Jesus tells us to ask God for our daily bread. When you study the word *bread* here, it did not just mean one loaf of bread. It meant give us today our bread and everything it takes to make it. In essence, He was telling us not just to pray for the "end benefit" but for everything that it takes to bring about the end product. In the case of bread, it's the sunlight, seeds, ground, harvesting, and baking. We are to put our trust in God that the whole process of our provision is blessed by Him.

Fourthly, Jesus tells us to ask God for forgiveness. As believers, we know that God has *already* forgiven us for our sins, and when we pray to God, we acknowledge this fact to our Father in Heaven. We are to thank Him for what Jesus did on the cross, which brought forgiveness of **ALL** sins. And because God forgave us, we are to live in the same spirit of forgiveness. We are to forgive our fellow man of everything they do to hurt us. Jesus made it very clear here that we are to forgive others as believers because, our Father has forgiven us.

Fifth, Jesus teaches us to ask God for direction so that we do not fall into temptation. We have an adversary; he is called here "the evil one." The devil's job is to steal, kill, and destroy a person's life (John 10:10). We cannot avoid the temptations of the evil one without God's direction. Think about this thought: Jesus was God, and He stilled ask His Heavenly Father for direction in regards to avoiding the temptations of the devil. Why? Because Jesus was God, but He was also man. His fleshly side was vulnerable to the sins of this world, and only God's leading can keep us from falling into sin. I have seen many people who tried to live life on their own and not trust God to keep them from falling into temptations, and each person eventually fell. For some people it took a week, others it took a month, some it took years, but their own will power ultimately failed them. This is the reason Jesus here shows us that we can go to God to find direction so we can navigate through the temptations of this world.

We have the right to stand boldly before the throne of God and ask what we will! This is one of our greatest assets, and we need to utilize it daily. Jesus spent hours in prayer daily. Why? Because He knew that He would not be able to accomplish His purpose here on earth without God's strength and direction. We must come to the same conclusion as Jesus did and develop a lifestyle of prayer. When we do, we will find the victory in life we are looking for. God promises it, so all we have to do is stand on His Word and pray!

As you study the scriptures on prayer, ask God to shed more light on the benefits of prayer and the lessons Jesus taught us about prayer. Develop a lifestyle of prayer, and you will see the benefits in your life.

Do you pray daily? How much time do you spend praying daily? Do you feel prayer is necessary?

Prayer Scriptures

(Philippians 4:6 NIV) Do not be anxious about anything, but in every situation, by prayer and petition, with thanksgiving, present your requests to God.

(1 Thessalonians 5:17 NIV) pray continually

(Mark 11:24 NIV) Therefore I tell you, whatever you ask for in prayer, believe that you have received it, and it will be yours

(Ephesians 6:18 NIV) And pray in the Spirit on all occasions with all kinds of prayers and requests. With this in mind, be alert and always keep on praying for all the Lord's people

(James 5:16 NIV) Therefore confess your sins to each other and pray for each other so that you may be healed. The prayer of a righteous person is powerful and effective

(Romans 8:26 NIV) In the same way, the Spirit helps us in our weakness. We do not know what we ought to pray for, but the Spirit himself intercedes for us through wordless groans

(John 15:7 NIV) If you remain in me and my words remain in you, ask whatever you wish, and it will be done for you.

(Matthew 21:22 NIV) If you believe, you will receive whatever you ask for in prayer."

(1 John 5:14-15 NIV) This is the confidence we have in approaching God: that if we ask anything according to his will, he hears us. [15] And if we know that he hears us—whatever we ask—we know that we have what we asked of him

(Matthew 6:7 NIV) And when you pray, do not keep on babbling like pagans, for they think they will be heard because of their many words.

(John 16:24 NIV) Until now you have not asked for anything in my name. Ask and you will receive, and your joy will be complete

(James 5:17 NIV) Elijah was a human being, even as we are. He prayed earnestly that it would not rain, and it did not rain on the land for three and a half years.

(Romans 8:26-27 NIV) In the same way, the Spirit helps us in our weakness. We do not know what we ought to pray for, but the Spirit himself intercedes for us through wordless groans. 27 And he who searches our heartsknows the mind of the Spirit, because the Spirit intercedes for God's people in accordance with the will of God.

(James 4:2 NIV) You desire but do not have, so you kill. You covet but you cannot get what you want, so you quarrel and fight. You do not have because you do not ask God

(Hebrews 11:6 NIV) And without faith it is impossible to please God, because anyone who comes to him must believe that he exists and that he rewards those who earnestly seek him.

(Ephesians 3:20 Now to him who is able to do immeasurably more than all we ask or imagine, according to his power that is at work within us,

(John 16:23 NIV) In that day you will no longer ask me anything. Very truly I tell you, my Father will give you whatever you ask in my name.

(Mark 9:29 NIV) He replied, "This kind can come out only by prayer.

(Matthew 26:36 NIV) Then Jesus went with his disciples to a place called Gethsemane, and he said to them, "Sit here while I go over there and pray."

(Matthew 7:7-11 NIV) "Ask and it will be given to you; seek and you will find; knock and the door will be opened to you.8 For everyone who asks receives; the one who seeks finds; and to the one who knocks, the door will be opened. 9 "Which of you, if your son asks for bread, will give him a stone? 10 Or if he asks for a fish, will give him a snake? 11 If you, then, though you are evil, know how to give good gifts to your children, how much more will your Father in heaven give good gifts to those who ask him!

(Matthew 5:44 NIV) But I tell you, love your enemies and pray for those who persecute you,

(Psalms 40:1 NIV) I waited patiently for the LORD; he turned to me and heard my cry

(2 Corinthians 1:9-11 NIV) Indeed, we felt we had received the sentence of death. But this happened that we might not rely on ourselves but on God, who raises the dead. 10 He has delivered us from such a deadly peril, and he will deliver us again. On him we have set our hope that he will continue to deliver us, 11 as you help us by your prayers. Then many will give thanks on our behalf for the gracious favor granted us in answer to the prayers of many.

(Romans 15:13 NIV) May the God of hope fill you with all joy and peace as you trust in him, so that you may overflow with hope by the power of the Holy Spirit.

(Romans 12:12 NIV) Be joyful in hope, patient in affliction, faithful in prayer.

(Romans 10:13 NIV) for, "Everyone who calls on the name of the Lord will be saved

(John 16:26 NIV) In that day you will ask in my name. I am not saying that I will ask the Father on your behalf.

(John 15:16 NIV) You did not choose me, but I chose you and appointed you so that you might go and bear fruit—fruit that will last—and so that whatever you ask in my name the Father will give you

(John 12:27 NIV) "Now my soul is troubled, and what shall I say? 'Father, save me from this hour'? No, it was for this very reason I came to this hour

(John 9:31 NIV) We know that God does not listen to sinners. He listens to the godly person who does his will.

(Luke 18:1 NIV) Then Jesus told his disciples a parable to show them that they should always pray and not give up.

(Mark 11:25 NIV) And when you stand praying, if you hold anything against anyone, forgive them, so that your Father in heaven may forgive you your sins."

(Mark 1:35 NIV) Very early in the morning, while it was still dark, Jesus got up, left the house and went off to a solitary place, where he prayed.

(Matthew 18:20 NIV) For where two or three gather in my name, there am I with them

(Matthew 6:5-13 NIV) "And when you pray, do not be like the hypocrites, for they love to pray standing in the synagogues and on the street corners to be seen by others. Truly I tell you, they have received their reward in full.[6] But when you pray, go into your room, close the door and pray to your Father, who is unseen. Then your Father, who sees what is done in secret, will reward you. [7] And when you pray, do not keep on babbling like pagans, for they think they will be heard because of their many words. [8] Do not be like them, for your Father knows what you need before you ask him. [9] "This, then, is how you should pray: 'Our Father in heaven, hallowed be your name, [10] your kingdom come, your will be done, on earth as it is in heaven. [11] Give us today our daily bread. [12] And forgive us our debts, as we also have forgiven our debtors. [13] And lead us not into temptation, but deliver us from the evil one.

(1 John 5:14 NIV) This is the confidence we have in approaching God: that if we ask anything according to his will, he hears us.

(James 1:5-7 NIV) If any of you lacks wisdom, you should ask God, who gives generously to all without finding fault, and it will be given to you. [6] But when you ask, you must believe and not doubt, because the one who doubts is like a wave of the sea, blown and tossed by the wind. [7] That person should not expect to receive anything from the Lord

(Hebrews 10:22-23 NIV) let us draw near to God with a sincere heart and with the full assurance that faith brings, having our hearts sprinkled to cleanse us from a guilty conscience and having our bodies washed with pure water. [23] Let us hold unswervingly to the hope we profess, for he who promised is faithful.

(Ephesians 6:18-20 NIV) And pray in the Spirit on all occasions with all kinds of prayers and requests. With this in mind, be alert and always keep on praying for all the Lord's people. [19] Pray also for me, that whenever I speak, words may be given me so that I will fearlessly make known the mystery of the gospel, [20] for which I am an ambassador in chains. Pray that I may declare it fearlessly, as I should.

Forgiveness

Colossians 1:13-14 – For he has rescued us from the dominion of darkness and brought us into the kingdom of the Son he loves, [14] in whom we have redemption, the forgiveness of sins. (NIV)

The realization and understanding of God's forgiveness in a person's life is life changing. Unfortunately, we live in an unforgiving world; people never let you forget the mistakes of your past. We watch in our news media here in the U.S. as countless athletes and celebrities make poor decisions, and they are portrayed as villains for the rest of their careers, even when they have done everything they could have done to remedy their mistakes. I am so glad to remind you today that God does not have the same standard of forgiveness as the world does. God decided to forgive us before we ever asked Him to (Romans 5:8). God sent His Son, Jesus Christ, into the world to pay the penalty price for the whole world's sins; and that price was death. Death was the sacrificial price for sin in order for mankind to have its relationship reestablished with God the Father. The greatest aspect of what Jesus accomplished on the cross was that we didn't do anything to deserve it. He loved us that much! He died for us so that we can have the abundance of God's grace flow into our lives and that we might receive the gift of righteousness so we can reign in life (Romans 5:17).

Colossians 1:13-14 tells us that God delivered us from the domain of darkness. Before we accepted Christ as our Lord and Savior, we lived in darkness. The original Greek word Paul uses here in this scripture is the word *"skotos,"* which comes from the root word *"skia,"* which means error or ignorance. Without revelation given by the Holy Spirit, we were ignorant of God's love for us, and we could never appreciate what Christ did for us on Calvary's cross. We lived in "the dark" about God's goodness and mercy. In Colossians, it goes on to say that we were transferred to the kingdom of His Son. When we are born again, we become citizens of

God's kingdom (Philippians 3:20). We now have an inheritance in heaven from God that

includes His forgiveness of all our mistakes and short comings! It doesn't matter what we do;

nothing is too great for God to forgive. That means if you have murdered, raped, stolen, lied,

cheated, lusted, or stressed yourself to the brink of death, God promises that He has **already**

forgiven you and **forgotten** all your lawless deeds (Hebrews 8:12). God's forgiveness is not

based on our self-righteousness or works. Nor is it dependent on other people's opinions! God's

forgiveness is based solely on His love for us!

As you study the scriptures on God's forgiveness, remember that you are forgiven. God

is not angry with you, because *ALL* of His anger towards sin was taken out on the body of

Jesus, the Christ. That is the victory you should be walking in every day. Do not live in

condemnation or guilt because God says we have nothing to feel condemned about because we

are in Christ Jesus (Romans 8:1). Continue to speak the Word of God over your life, and remind

yourself daily that you are the righteousness of God through Christ (2 Corinthians 5:21).

Do you still feel guilty and condemned about the sins of your past?

Forgiveness Scriptures

(Hebrews 4:16 NLT) Let us therefore come boldly to the throne of grace, that we may obtain mercy and find grace to help in time of need.

(Matthew 11:28 NLT) Then Jesus said, "Come to me, all of you who are weary and carry heavy burdens, and I will give you rest.

(Psalm 55:22 NLT) Give your burdens to the LORD, and he will take care of you. He will not permit the godly to slip and fall.

(1 John 2:1 NLT) My dear children, I am writing this to you so that you will not sin. But if anyone does sin, we have an advocate who pleads our case before the Father. He is Jesus Christ, the one who is truly righteous

(1 John 1:9 NLT) But if we confess our sins to him, he is faithful and just to forgive us our sins and to cleanse us from all wickedness

(Acts 3:19 NLT) Now repent of your sins and turn to God, so that your sins may be wiped away.

(Isaiah 43:25-26 NLT) "I — yes, I alone — will blot out your sins for my own sake and will never think of them again. [26] Let us review the situation together, and you can present your case to prove your innocence

(Romans 8:1 NLT) So now there is no condemnation for those who belong to Christ Jesus.

(Isaiah 1:18 NLT) "Come now, let's settle this," says the LORD. "Though your sins are like scarlet, I will make them as white as snow. Though they are red like crimson, I will make them as white as wool.

(2 Corinthians 5:17 NLT) This means that anyone who belongs to Christ has become a new person. The old life is gone; a new life has begun!

(Ephesian 1:7 NLT) He is so rich in kindness and grace that he purchased our freedom with the blood of his Son and forgave our sins.

(Psalm 32:5 NLT) Finally, I confessed all my sins to you and stopped trying to hide my guilt. I said to myself, "I will confess my rebellion to the LORD." And you forgave me! All my guilt is gone.

(Psalm 79:9 NLT) Help us, O God of our salvation! Help us for the glory of your name. Save us and forgive our sins for the honor of your name.

(Matthew 26:28 NLT) for this is my blood, which confirms the covenant between God and his people. It is poured out as a sacrifice to forgive the sins of many.

Salvation

Romans 10:9-10 — That if thou shalt confess with thy mouth the Lord Jesus, and shalt believe in thine heart that God hath raised him from the dead, thou shalt be saved. For with the heart man believeth unto righteousness; and with the mouth confession is made unto salvation. (KJV)

Salvation is the greatest gift God has given to a believer. In a world filled with so much heartache and pain, at times it is comforting to know that when we leave this earth, we will spend eternity in heaven with our Lord Jesus Christ, because we are saved! Because of our salvation, we know what our future holds, and it gives us strength to live in this life. Those who are not saved do not have this security; they are solely dependent of their own self-efforts to make it through life. The major problem they face is that once their life is over, none of their works would qualify them for heaven. The only qualifying factor God looks at to enter into heaven is our acceptance of His Son Jesus Christ, through faith, as our Lord and Savior. Our salvation has nothing to do with our works but only the finished work of Jesus on the cross!

Understanding the benefits of our salvation is the key to successful living. When we pray the prayer of salvation that Paul taught us about in Romans 10:9, *"That if thou shalt confess with thy mouth the Lord Jesus, and shalt believe in thine heart that God hath raised him from the dead, thou shalt be saved,"* we are what Jesus called "born again" (John 3:3). We are born into a new life full of God's grace! The old person that we were before our acceptance of Jesus is dead, and we are a new creation through Christ Jesus (2 Corinthians 5:17). This is the good news of our salvation; we belong to God, and He promises to take care of us while we are here on earth and after in heaven.

As you study the verses on salvation, remember that God's salvation comes with a guarantee of heaven after we die, and it comes with God's blessing on our lives here on earth. Speak God's Word over your life daily, and continue to pray that God reveals *all* of the benefits that come along with His salvation to you.

Do you know without a shadow of a doubt that you are saved? Do you encourage others to become born again as you are?

Salvation Scriptures

(Ephesians 2:8-9 KJV) For by grace are ye saved through faith; and that not of yourselves: it is the gift of God: 9 Not of works, lest any man should boast.

(Mark 10:25-27) It is easier for a camel to go through the eye of a needle, than for a rich man to enter into the kingdom of God. [26] And they were astonished out of measure, saying among themselves, Who then can be saved? [27] And Jesus looking upon them saith, With men it is impossible, but not with God: for with God all things are possible.

(Romans 3:20 KJV) Therefore by the deeds of the law there shall no flesh be justified in his sight: for by the law is the knowledge of sin.

(Romans 11:6 KJV) And if by grace, then is it no more of works: otherwise grace is no more grace. But if it be of works, then is it no more grace: otherwise work is no more work.

(Galatians 2:16 KJV) "Knowing that a man is not justified by the works of the law, but by the faith of Jesus Christ, even we have believed in Jesus Christ, that we might be justified by the faith of Christ, and not by the works of the law: for by the works of the law shall no flesh be justified.

(2 Timothy 1:9 KJV) Who hath saved us, and called us with an holy calling, not according to our works, but according to his own purpose and grace, which was given us in Christ Jesus before the world began,

(Titus 3:5 KJV) Not by works of righteousness which we have done, but according to his mercy he saved us, by the washing of regeneration, and renewing of the Holy Ghost;

(Acts 4:12 KJV) Neither is there salvation in any other: for there is none other name under heaven given among men, whereby we must be saved.

(1 Timothy 2:5 KJV) "For there is one God, and one mediator between God and men, the man Christ Jesus;

(John 3:16 KJV) For God so loved the world, that he gave his only begotten Son, that whosoever believeth in him should not perish, but have everlasting life.

(John 3:36 KJV) He that believeth on the Son hath everlasting life: and he that believeth not the Son shall not see life; but the wrath of God abideth on him.

(John 8:24 KJV) I said therefore unto you, that ye shall die in your sins: for if ye believe not that I am he, ye shall die in your sins.

(John 10:1 KJV) Verily, verily, I say unto you, He that entereth not by the door into the sheepfold, but climbeth up some other way, the same is a thief and a robber.

(John 10:9 KJV) I am the door: by me if any man enter in, he shall be saved, and shall go in and out, and find pasture.

(John 14:6 KJV) Jesus saith unto him, I am the way, the truth, and the life: no man cometh unto the Father, but by me.

(1 Corinthians 3:11 KJV) For other foundation can no man lay than that is laid, which is Jesus Christ.

(1 John 5:12 KJV) He that hath the Son hath life; and he that hath not the Son of God hath not life.

(Revelation 3:20 KJV) Behold, I stand at the door, and knock: if any man hear my voice, and open the door, I will come in to him, and will sup with him, and he with me.

(John 1:12 KJV) But as many as received him, to them gave he power to become the sons of God, even to them that believe on his name:

(Ephesians 3:17 KJV) That Christ may dwell in your hearts by faith; that ye, being rooted and grounded in love,

(Romans 6:23 KJV) For the wages of sin is death; but the gift of God is eternal life through Jesus Christ our Lord.

(John 11:26 KJV) And whosoever liveth and believeth in me shall never die. Believest thou this?

(John 14:2-3 KJV) In my Father's house are many mansions: if it were not so, I would have told you. I go to prepare a place for you. ³And if I go and prepare a place for you, I will come again, and receive you unto myself; that where I am, there ye may be also.

(1 Peter 1:3-4 KJV) Blessed be the God and Father of our Lord Jesus Christ, which according to his abundant mercy hath begotten us again unto a lively hope by the resurrection of Jesus Christ from the dead, ⁴To an inheritance incorruptible, and undefiled, and that fadeth not away, reserved in heaven for you,

Favor

Psalm 90:17 — May the favor of the Lord our God rest upon us; establish the work of our hands for us —

yes, establish the work of our hands. (NIV)

Finding favor with a person that has significant influence in society is a good thing to have. People spend thousands of dollars each year to join country clubs and private communities in order to be able to network with people in power or position. Finding favor with people is the source of many business's cash flow and overall survival. With favor being so vital to a person's success, we as believers have a great promise from our God that says we have favor with Him at all times.

Favor with God is better than having favor with the richest person on earth. It is also more valuable than having favor with the strongest political leader on the earth. Why? Because God created and owns *everything* (Psalm 24:1). As believers, our Heavenly Father owns everything we see every day. All of the material things we strive for belong to God. Even the connections we desire to make for our careers, businesses, or organizations are available to us because we find favor with God.

David, in Psalm 90:17, says, "*May the favor of the Lord our God rest upon us; establish the work of our hands for us — yes, establish the work of our hands.*" If anyone knew about God's favor, it was King David. God showed David favor when He chose David to be king while he was still a young boy (1 Samuel 16:11-13). And God showed David favor when he fought the giant Goliath (1 Samuel 17). All throughout David's life he saw the favor of God rest on him. All throughout the Psalms that David wrote, he constantly praised God for bringing him and his family through unimaginable situations.

The good news is that the same God that showed David so much favor desires to do the same for *ALL* believers today! God is a God who desires the best for His people, and He will always keep His Word (Numbers 23:19). You have God's favor on your life, so you can walk in confidence each day that whatever door you need open or resource you need supplied, God is faithful to provide for **ALL** your needs according to His riches and glory in Christ Jesus (Philippians 4:19).

As you study the scriptures on God's favor, remember to speak the Word of God over your life each day. God promised to show you favor, so your faith should always be in His Word and not what your situation looks like.

Do you believe God favors you? In what ways has God shown you His favor in the past year?

Favor Scriptures

(Gen. 6:8 NIV) But Noah found favor in the eyes of the LORD.

Gen. 18:3 NIV) He said, "If I have found favor in your eyes, my lord, do not pass your servant by.

(Gen. 19:19 NIV)Your servant has found favor in your eyes, and you have shown great kindness to me in sparing my life. But I can't flee to the mountains; this disaster will overtake me, and I'll die.

(Gen. 39:21 NIV) the LORD was with him; he showed him kindness and granted him favor in the eyes of the prison warden.

(Ex. 33:13 NIV) If you are pleased with me, teach me your ways so I may know you and continue to find favor with you. Remember that this nation is your people."

(Ex. 34:9 NIV) "O Lord, if I have found favor in your eyes," he said, "then let the Lord go with us. Although this is a stiff-necked people, forgive our wickedness and our sin, and take us as your inheritance."

(Lev. 26:9 NIV) "'I will look on you with favor and make you fruitful and increase your numbers, and I will keep my covenant with you.

(Deut. 33:16 NIV) with the best gifts of the earth and its fullness and the favor of him who dwelt in the burning bush. Let all these rest on the head of Joseph, on the brow of the prince among his brothers.

(Ezra 7:28 NIV) and who has extended his good favor to me before the king and his advisers and all the king's powerful officials. Because the hand of the LORD my God was on me, I took courage and gathered leading men from Israel to go up with me.

(Job 33:26 NIV) He prays to God and finds favor with him, he sees God's face and shouts for joy; he is restored by God to his righteous state.

(Psa. 5:12 NIV) For surely, O LORD, you bless the righteous; you surround them with your favor as with a shield.

(Psa. 30:5 NIV) For his anger lasts only a moment, but his favor lasts a lifetime; weeping may remain for a night, but rejoicing comes in the morning.

(Psa. 69:13 NIV) But I pray to you, O LORD, in the time of your favor; in your great love, O God, answer me with your sure salvation.

(Psa. 90:17 NIV) May the favor of the Lord our God rest upon us; establish the work of our hands for us — yes, establish the work of our hands.

(Psa. 102:13 NIV) You will arise and have compassion on Zion, for it is time to show favor to her; the appointed time has come.

(Proverbs 3:3-4 NIV) Let love and faithfulness never leave you; bind them around your neck, write them on the tablet of your heart. 4Then you will win favor and a good name in the sight of God and man.

(Prov. 13:15 NIV) Good understanding wins favor, but the way of the unfaithful is hard

(Luke 2:52 NIV) And Jesus grew in wisdom and stature, and in favor with God and men.

(Luke 2:52 NIV) And Jesus grew in wisdom and stature, and in favor with God and men.

(John 5:32 NIV) There is another who testifies in my favor, and I know that his testimony about me is valid.

(Acts 7:46 NIV) who enjoyed God's favor and asked that he might provide a dwelling place for the God of Jacob.

(2Cor. 6:2 NIV) For he says, "In the time of my favor I heard you, and in the day of salvation I helped you." I tell you, now is the time of God's favor, now is the day of salvation.

Holy Spirit

John 15:26 — "When the Advocate comes, whom I will send to you from the Father — the Spirit of truth who goes out from the Father — he will testify about me." (NIV)

A person interviewing for a good job, or someone dealing with a lawsuit, looks for people that can be a good advocate for them. An advocate is someone that speaks or writes in support of a person or a cause. The person interviewing for a new job needs an advocate, which is commonly called a reference. This is a person who the potential employer can call to learn more about the person interviewing for the job. The advocate brings credibility to the interviewer's resume, because they can testify of the legitimacy of the interviewer's experience, education, or intangible skills. They become a vital part of the process during which an employer decides to hire or pass on a candidate. The Bible tells us that the Holy Spirit is the advocate sent by God to testify and reveal the person of Christ Jesus.

The benefit for us having the Holy Spirit as an advocate is that He teaches us who Christ is, which in turn shows us who we are in Christ. The Holy Spirit empowers us to live as Christ lived and to accomplish the assignment God placed on our lives before the beginning of time. It is important to note that Jesus did not begin His ministry until He was filled with the Holy Spirit (Matthew 3:16). As believers, when we accepted Christ as our Lord and Savior, the same Holy Spirit who empowered Jesus now empowers each of us! The Holy Spirit teaches us, comforts us, and guides us in the way God will have us to go.

The good news is that we are not alone ever! We have the Holy Spirit living on the inside of us sitting there ready and available to us 24/7 & 365. We have the right to walk through life in total confidence, because we know that we have *supernatural* power within us.

As we see problems come into our lives, we can be encouraged because we know that no problem is too big for our God and He sent us an advocate who will be there to guide us through any situation. Jesus even tells us in John 16:7: *"But very truly I tell you, it is for your good that I am going away. Unless I go away, the Advocate will not come to you; but if I go, I will send him to you."*

As you can see, it was in our best interests for the Advocate to come. Why did Jesus say this? The reason was simple. While Jesus was on earth, He lived in a human body with all its limitations. So, if people wanted to learn from Jesus, they would have to travel to wherever He was. Dependent on where Jesus was on any given day, you may or may not have been able to get to Him. Jesus could only be in one place at one time. But when He went away, the Holy Spirit, who was not limited to an earthly body, could be omnipresent. The Holy Spirit could teach everyone all around the world about the person of Christ Jesus and empower them to live life victoriously! The Holy Spirit is our great enabler, and He is one of the best benefits we have as believers.

As you study the scriptures on the Holy Spirit, remember that He is with you every day. You are never alone; you have a comforter who will be there to help you with whatever you need. Meditate on God's Word daily and allow the Holy Spirit to lead you in all your endeavors.

Do you allow the Holy Spirit to lead you in your decisions?

Holy Spirit Scriptures

(Matthew 1:18 NIV) This is how the birth of Jesus the Messiah came about[a]: His mother Mary was pledged to be married to Joseph, but before they came together, she was found to be pregnant through the Holy Spirit.

(Matthew 28:19 NIV) Therefore go and make disciples of all nations, baptizing them in the name of the Father and of the Son and of the Holy Spirit,

(John 14:16 NIV) And I will ask the Father, and he will give you another advocate to help you and be with you forever

(John 14:26 NIV) But the Advocate, the Holy Spirit, whom the Father will send in my name, will teach you all things and will remind you of everything I have said to you.

(Acts 1:8 NIV) But you will receive power when the Holy Spirit comes on you; and you will be my witnesses in Jerusalem, and in all Judea and Samaria, and to the ends of the earth."

(Romans 5:5 NIV) And hope does not put us to shame, because God's love has been poured out into our hearts through the Holy Spirit, who has been given to us.

(Mark 13:11 NIV) Whenever you are arrested and brought to trial, do not worry beforehand about what to say. Just say whatever is given you at the time, for it is not you speaking, but the Holy Spirit.

(Acts 2:38 NIV) Peter replied, "Repent and be baptized, every one of you, in the name of Jesus Christ for the forgiveness of your sins. And you will receive the gift of the Holy Spirit.

(Romans 8:26 NIV) In the same way, the Spirit helps us in our weakness. We do not know what we ought to pray for, but the Spirit himself intercedes for us through wordless groans. [27] And he who searches our hearts knows the mind of the Spirit, because the Spirit intercedes for God's people in accordance with the will of God.

(1Corinthians 12:4 NIV) There are different kinds of gifts, but the same Spirit distributes them.

(1Corinthians 12:11 NIV) All these are the work of one and the same Spirit, and he distributes them to each one, just as he determines.

(Ephesians 4:30 NIV) And do not grieve the Holy Spirit of God, with whom you were sealed for the day of redemption.

(1John 5:7 NIV) For there are three that testify: [8] the Spirit, the water and the blood; and the three are in agreement.

(Acts 9:31 NIV) Then the church throughout Judea, Galilee and Samaria enjoyed a time of peace and was strengthened. Living in the fear of the Lord and encouraged by the Holy Spirit, it increased in numbers.

(Luke 3:22 NIV) and the Holy Spirit descended on him in bodily form like a dove. And a voice came from heaven: "You are my Son, whom I love; with you I am well pleased."

(Acts 2:1-4 NIV) When the day of Pentecost came, they were all together in one place. ²Suddenly a sound like the blowing of a violent wind came from heaven and filled the whole house where they were sitting.³ They saw what seemed to be tongues of fire that separated and came to rest on each of them. ⁴ All of them were filled with the Holy Spirit and began to speak in other tongues[a] as the Spirit enabled them.

(Luke 11:13 NIV) If you then, though you are evil, know how to give good gifts to your children, how much more will your Father in heaven give the Holy Spirit to those who ask him!"

(John 7:39 NIV) By this he meant the Spirit, whom those who believed in him were later to receive. Up to that time the Spirit had not been given, since Jesus had not yet been glorified.

(1Corinthians 2:13 NIV) This is what we speak, not in words taught us by human wisdom but in words taught by the Spirit, explaining spiritual realities with Spirit-taught words.

Inheritance

Ephesians 1:11 — Furthermore, because we are united with Christ, we have received an inheritance from

God, for he chose us in advance, and he makes everything work out according to his plan. (NLT)

Many people are born rich because of an inheritance left by their ancestors, while others work hard each day trying to leave some type of inheritance for their children and grandchildren. Leaving an inheritance for your family is one of the most honorable deeds you can do, and the Bible even attests to this point: Proverbs 13:22 — **A good person leaves an inheritance for their children's children, but a sinner's wealth is stored up for the righteous (NIV).** If man can do a great deed and leave an inheritance for his children, then what should we expect from our Heavenly Father? Our Father in Heaven is a good father, and His Word says that we as believers have an inheritance.

Ephesians 1:11 tells us that since we have become united with Christ, we **have** received an inheritance from God. The key words in the verse are, "**have received.**" Notice that the verse did not say, "will receive." The verse says, "have received." This is a critical point for us as believers to understand, because many believers go through life "waiting" for their inheritance. But the Word of God says we have already received our inheritance! The problem is that we have not seen it totally materialized yet, because we have not had the faith to ask for it. Why? Because many believers think that they will only receive their inheritance in heaven after they die.

While it is true that we will receive part of our inheritance in heaven, there are things that God wants us to experience here on earth! When you study the life of Christ, you will see that everywhere He went people were healed, fed, set free from bondage, and even raised from the dead. The life of Christ revealed to us part of the inheritance we would receive from the Father once we accepted Him as our Lord and Savior. The Bible is filled with what God desires for us while we are still here on earth. Our inheritance includes the Holy Spirit's empowerment, knowledge of the mysteries of God, wisdom, good health, prosperity, peace, the opportunity to become a son or daughter of God, and joy to name a few.

If your parents never left you an inheritance to live on, know that your Heavenly Father did! You have an inheritance available to you right now, and all you have to do is access it by faith. You do not have to earn it or work for it in any type of way. Christ finished the work for us all, and now we can experience the inheritance our Heavenly Father purposed for us from the beginning of time (Ephesians 1:11). As you study the scriptures on your inheritance in God, remember to speak the Word of God over your life every day. Ask the Holy Spirit to lead you in your understanding so that you can see the full manifestation of your inheritance while you are still here on earth.

Do you depend on your own resources or your inheritance given by God?

Inheritance Scriptures

(Proverbs 13:22 ESV) A good man leaves an inheritance to his children's children, but the sinner's wealth is laid up for the righteous.

(Ephesians 1:11-14 ESV) In him we have obtained an inheritance, having been predestined according to the purpose of him who works all things according to the counsel of his will, so that we who were the first to hope in Christ might be to the praise of his glory. In him you also, when you heard the word of truth, the gospel of your salvation, and believed in him, were sealed with the promised Holy Spirit, who is the guarantee of our inheritance until we acquire possession of it, to the praise of his glory.

(Ephesians 1:18 ESV) Having the eyes of your hearts enlightened, that you may know what is the hope to which he has called you, what are the riches of his glorious inheritance in the saints,

(Colossians 3:23-24 ESV) Whatever you do, work heartily, as for the Lord and not for men, knowing that from the Lord you will receive the inheritance as your reward. You are serving the Lord Christ.

(Psalm 37:29 ESV) The righteous shall inherit the land and dwell upon it forever.

(Proverbs 20:21 ESV) An inheritance gained hastily in the beginning will not be blessed in the end.

(Titus 3:7 ESV) So that being justified by his grace we might become heirs according to the hope of eternal life.

(Acts 20:32 ESV) And now I commend you to God and to the word of his grace, which is able to build you up and to give you the inheritance among all those who are sanctified.

(Romans 8:17 ESV) And if children, then heirs—heirs of God and fellow heirs with Christ, provided we suffer with him in order that we may also be glorified with him.

(Psalm 16:6 ESV) The lines have fallen for me in pleasant places; indeed, I have a beautiful inheritance.

(Proverbs 17:2 ESV) A servant who deals wisely will rule over a son who acts shamefully and will share the inheritance as one of the brothers.

(Psalm 2:7-8 ESV) I will tell of the decree: The Lord said to me, "You are my Son; today I have begotten you. Ask of me, and I will make the nations your heritage, and the ends of the earth your possession.

(Joshua 14:9 ESV) And Moses swore on that day, saying, 'Surely the land on which your foot has trodden shall be an inheritance for you and your children forever, because you have wholly followed the Lord my God.'

(1 Peter 5:6-7 ESV) Humble yourselves, therefore, under the mighty hand of God so that at the proper time he may exalt you, casting all your anxieties on him, because he cares for you.

(Hebrews 1:2 ESV) But in these last days he has spoken to us by his Son, whom he appointed the heir of all things, through whom also he created the world.

(Galatians 4:1-7 ESV) I mean that the heir, as long as he is a child, is no different from a slave, though he is the owner of everything, [2] but he is under guardians and managers until the date set by his father. [3] In the same way we also, when we were children, were enslaved to the elementary principles[b] of the world.[4] But when the fullness of time had come, God sent forth his Son, born of woman, born under the law,[5] to redeem those who were under the law, so that we might receive adoption as sons. [6] And because you are sons, God has sent the Spirit of his Son into our hearts, crying, "Abba! Father!" [7] So you are no longer a slave, but a son, and if a son, then an heir through God.

(Colossians 1:12 ESV) Giving thanks to the Father, who has qualified you to share in the inheritance of the saints in light.

(Matthew 6:25-34 ESV) "Therefore I tell you, do not be anxious about your life, what you will eat or what you will drink, nor about your body, what you will put on. Is not life more than food, and the body more than clothing?[26] Look at the birds of the air: they neither sow nor reap nor gather into barns, and yet your heavenly Father feeds them. Are you not of more value than they? [27] And which of you by being anxious can add a single hour to his span of life? [28] And why are you anxious about clothing? Consider the lilies of the field, how they grow: they neither toil nor spin, [29] yet I tell you, even Solomon in all his glory was not arrayed like one of these. [30] But if God so clothes the grass of the field, which today is alive and tomorrow is thrown into the oven, will he not much more clothe you, O you of little faith?[31] Therefore do not be anxious, saying, 'What shall we eat?' or 'What shall we drink?' or 'What shall we wear?' [32] For the Gentiles seek after all these things, and your heavenly Father knows that you need them all. [33] But seek first the kingdom of God and his righteousness, and all these things will be added to you. [34] "Therefore do not be anxious about tomorrow, for tomorrow will be anxious for itself. Sufficient for the day is its own trouble.

(Proverbs 11:29 ESV) Whoever troubles his own household will inherit the wind, and the fool will be servant to the wise of heart.

(Genesis 25:5 ESV) Abraham gave all he had to Isaac.

(2 Timothy 3:16-17 ESV) All Scripture is breathed out by God and profitable for teaching, for reproof, for correction, and for training in righteousness, that the man of God may be competent, equipped for every good work.

(Psalm 127:4 ESV) Like arrows in the hand of a warrior are the children of one's youth.

(Psalm 16:5 ESV) The Lord is my chosen portion and my cup; you hold my lot.

Grace

Ephesians 2:8 — For it is by grace you have been saved, through faith — and this is not from yourselves, it is the gift of God. (NIV)

God's grace is one of the most misunderstood elements of a believer's relationship with God. We live in a world that is unforgiving, cold, and harsh. And unfortunately, we experience so much of these characteristics daily that we unknowingly take the systems of the world into our relationship with our Heavenly Father. Because the world is unforgiving, we tend to look at God as unforgiving. Because the world is cold, we think God also is cold. And this type of thinking leaves the believer stressed, worried, and depleted. We must understand that our relationship with God has nothing to do with how "good" we are. It has everything to do with how "good" He is. It is by the grace of God we are saved through faith in His Son Jesus Christ.

God's grace is a gift from God. The Bible says that we are under the new covenant of grace. This covenant has nothing to do with our works, nor does it have anything to do with us "earning" God's salvation. This new covenant had everything to do with God and His decision to make us His people and to put us in right standing with Himself (Hebrews 8:6-13 & Jeremiah 31:31-37). God's abundance of grace came through the death of Jesus Christ on the cross (Romans 5:17). Forgiveness for the sins of the world was given by God through His Son, and it was our responsibility to receive it. This was God's grace! He covered all of our mistakes and weaknesses. Jesus fulfilled the law for us so that we could stand before God in boldness by faith in the finished work of Jesus Christ.

The Bible tells us we are no longer under the law, and by grace, we are made righteous before God. This does not mean we can go out and sin as much as we want (Romans 6:1-2). But it does mean that if we do have a moment of weakness and commit a sin, God's grace is there to cover us! We can point to the cross of Jesus and say we are forgiven! God's grace released us from the bondage of condemnation and guilt (Romans 8:1), and we can live in the freedom God desired for us.

This freedom releases us to go before God in prayer by faith; it releases us to have joy, peace, and healing. This is the covenant we are under, and as believers, we need to remember to walk in its freedoms each day and not think of God as some kind of task master who only responds kindly to us if we do "good." The truth is that God demonstrated His love towards us while we were in the mist of our sins, Christ died for us (Romans 5:8). God's blessings towards us have nothing to do with us but what His will is. And the Bible tells us that His will for us is that we prosper and have hope and good success (Jeremiah 29:11).

As you study the scriptures on God's grace, remember that Jesus finished the work of the cross. He fulfilled the law on our behalf, and we cannot earn God's blessing, but we receive it through faith in Jesus Christ. It is by God's grace we are made righteous before God and not of ourselves. When you make mistakes, you do not have to be condemned and live with the guilt. Christ came and died so that you can be free! You are free in Christ, and you have the right to walk in it each day for the rest of your life. Remember to speak the Word of God over your life daily and allow the Holy Spirit to teach you the full depth of God's grace.

Do you walk in God's grace? Or do you live with the condemnation and guilt of your past?

Grace Scriptures

(Ephesians 2:8 ESV) For by grace you have been saved through faith. And this is not your own doing; it is the gift of God,

(2 Timothy 2:1-2 ESV) You then, my child, be strengthened by the grace that is in Christ Jesus, and what you have heard from me in the presence of many witnesses entrust to faithful men who will be able to teach others also.

(Romans 11:6 ESV) But if it is by grace, it is no longer on the basis of works; otherwise grace would no longer be grace.

(Acts 20:24 ESV) But I do not account my life of any value nor as precious to myself, if only I may finish my course and the ministry that I received from the Lord Jesus, to testify to the gospel of the grace of God.

(Hebrews 4:16 ESV) Let us then with confidence draw near to the throne of grace, that we may receive mercy and find grace to help in time of need.

(2 Corinthians 12:9-12 ESV) But he said to me, "My grace is sufficient for you, for my power is made perfect in weakness." Therefore I will boast all the more gladly of my weaknesses, so that the power of Christ may rest upon me. For the sake of Christ, then, I am content with weaknesses, insults, hardships, persecutions, and calamities. For when I am weak, then I am strong. I have been a fool! You forced me to it, for I ought to have been commended by you. For I was not at all inferior to these super-apostles, even though I am nothing. The signs of a true apostle were performed among you with utmost patience, with signs and wonders and mighty works.

(Romans 6:23 ESV) For the wages of sin is death, but the free gift of God is eternal life in Christ Jesus our Lord.

(John 1:12 ESV) But to all who did receive him, who believed in his name, he gave the right to become children of God,

(1 John 4:19 ESV) We love because he first loved us.

(Romans 10:9 ESV) Because, if you confess with your mouth that Jesus is Lord and believe in your heart that God raised him from the dead, you will be saved.

(Malachi 3:17 ESV) "They shall be mine, says the Lord of hosts, in the day when I make up my treasured possession, and I will spare them as a man spares his son who serves him.

(Acts 2:38 ESV) And Peter said to them, "Repent and be baptized every one of you in the name of Jesus Christ for the forgiveness of your sins, and you will receive the gift of the Holy Spirit.

(John 15:16 ESV) You did not choose me, but I chose you and appointed you that you should go and bear fruit and that your fruit should abide, so that whatever you ask the Father in my name, he may give it to you.

(John 5:24 ESV) Truly, truly, I say to you, whoever hears my word and believes him who sent me has eternal life. He does not come into judgment, but has passed from death to life.

(John 3:16 ESV) "For God so loved the world, that he gave his only Son, that whoever believes in him should not perish but have eternal life.

(John 14:6 ESV) Jesus said to him, "I am the way, and the truth, and the life. No one comes to the Father except through me.

(John 10:9 ESV) I am the door. If anyone enters by me, he will be saved and will go in and out and find pasture.

Confidence

Philippians 4:13 – I can do all things through Christ which strengtheneth me. (KJV)

Confidence is said to be a necessary quality to be successful in life. Employers look for confident candidates to fill positions, countries seek out confident men and women to run their nations, and men and women both look for confidence in a person they are dating before they decide to take the next step in their relationship. Confidence, it seems, is essential for survival and success here on earth, and as believers, we should be the most confident people there are. Our confidence does not stem from our own abilities, resources, education, or networks. Our confidence comes from God and what He blessed us with!

One of the greatest scriptures on the source of a believer's confidence can be found in Philippians 4:13: I can do all things through Christ which strengtheneth me. Paul here reveals to us where our strength as believers comes from. Our strength comes from Christ! The benefit of this verse to us can be found in the understanding and knowledge of who Christ is. Christ was man and yet still God (Philippians 2:6). With this knowledge, we know that God is all powerful, and no one or nothing can stand against Him. And with God on our side, nothing can stand against us (Romans 8:31). Christ is our source of strength, and that means we have an unlimited amount of strength, because our source **never** runs out! We can walk confidently in life, because we have the person who created and owns everything on our side. This should bring confidence to the believer! We do not have to live in fear of anything, because God's got our back. We can stand tall and speak loud without any shyness because of who our daddy is. Our daddy is the King of kings and Lord of lords (Revelations 19:16). And He desires that we live life in this confidence.

As you study the scriptures on confidence, remember to speak the Word of God over your life daily. You have the right to walk in confidence every day no matter what your bank account looks like, no matter what family you were born into, and no matter what mistakes you made in life. Your confidence comes through Christ Jesus which strengthens you!

Do you live life with confidence? What areas in your life aren't you confident about?

Confidence Scriptures

(Philippians 4:13 ESV) I can do all things through him who strengthens me.

(2 Timothy 1:7 ESV) For God gave us a spirit not of fear but of power and love and self-control.

(Hebrews 13:6 ESV) So we can confidently say, "The Lord is my helper; I will not fear; what can man do to me?"

(Hebrews 10:35-36 ESV) Therefore do not throw away your confidence, which has a great reward. For you have need of endurance, so that when you have done the will of God you may receive what is promised.

(Psalm 139:13-14 ESV) For you formed my inward parts; you knitted me together in my mother's womb. I praise you, for I am fearfully and wonderfully made. Wonderful are your works; my soul knows it very well.

(Psalm 27:3 ESV) Though an army encamp against me, my heart shall not fear; though war arise against me, yet I will be confident.

(Joshua 1:9 ESV) Have I not commanded you? Be strong and courageous. Do not be frightened, and do not be dismayed, for the Lord your God is with you wherever you go."

(Proverbs 3:6 ESV) In all your ways acknowledge him, and he will make straight your paths.

(1 John 4:18 ESV) There is no fear in love, but perfect love casts out fear. For fear has to do with punishment, and whoever fears has not been perfected in love.

(Galatians 2:20 ESV) I have been crucified with Christ. It is no longer I who live, but Christ who lives in me. And the life I now live in the flesh I live by faith in the Son of God, who loved me and gave himself for me.

(Philippians 4:4-7 ESV) Rejoice in the Lord always; again I will say, Rejoice. Let your reasonableness be known to everyone. The Lord is at hand; do not be anxious about anything, but in everything by prayer and supplication with thanksgiving let your requests be made known to God. And the peace of God, which surpasses all understanding, will guard your hearts and your minds in Christ Jesus.

(Philippians 1:6 ESV) And I am sure of this, that he who began a good work in you will bring it to completion at the day of Jesus Christ.

(Psalm 91:1-2 ESV) He who dwells in the shelter of the Most High will abide in the shadow of the Almighty. I will say to the Lord, "My refuge and my fortress, my God, in whom I trust

(Matthew 6:34 ESV) "Therefore do not be anxious about tomorrow, for tomorrow will be anxious for itself. Sufficient for the day is its own trouble.

(2 Corinthians 12:9 ESV) But he said to me, "My grace is sufficient for you, for my power is made perfect in weakness." Therefore I will boast all the more gladly of my weaknesses, so that the power of Christ may rest upon me.

(1 Corinthians 2:3-5 ESV) And I was with you in weakness and in fear and much trembling, and my speech and my message were not in plausible words of wisdom, but in demonstration of the Spirit and of power, that your faith might not rest in the wisdom of men but in the power of God.

(Hebrews 4:16 ESV) Let us then with confidence draw near to the throne of grace, that we may receive mercy and find grace to help in time of need.

(Romans 8:28 ESV) And we know that for those who love God all things work together for good, for those who are called according to his purpose.

(James 1:12 ESV) Blessed is the man who remains steadfast under trial, for when he has stood the test he will receive the crown of life, which God has promised to those who love him.

(1 Timothy 4:12 ESV) Let no one despise you for your youth, but set the believers an example in speech, in conduct, in love, in faith, in purity.

(Proverbs 29:25 ESV) The fear of man lays a snare, but whoever trusts in the Lord is safe.

(2 Peter 1:3 ESV) His divine power has granted to us all things that pertain to life and godliness, through the knowledge of him who called us to his own glory and excellence,

(Psalm 23:1-6 ESV) The LORD is my shepherd; I shall not want. 2He makes me lie down in green pastures. He leads me beside still waters. 3 He restores my soul. He leads me in paths of righteousness for his name's sake. 4 Even though I walk through the valley of the shadow of death, I will fear no evil, for you are with me; your rod and your staff, they comfort me. 5 You prepare a table before me in the presence of my enemies; you anoint my head with oil; my cup overflows. 6 Surely goodness and mercy shall follow me all the days of my life, and I shall dwell[1] in the house of the LORD forever.

(Psalm 27:1-2 ESV) Of David. The Lord is my light and my salvation; whom shall I fear? The Lord is the stronghold of my life; of whom shall I be afraid? When evildoers assail me to eat up my flesh, my adversaries and foes, it is they who stumble and fall.

(John 3:16 ESV) "For God so loved the world, that he gave his only Son, that whoever believes in him should not perish but have eternal life.

(Jeremiah 17:7-8 ESV) "Blessed is the man who trusts in the Lord, whose trust is the Lord. He is like a tree planted by water, that sends out its roots by the stream, and does not fear when heat comes, for its leaves remain green, and is not anxious in the year of drought, for it does not cease to bear fruit."

(Acts 1:8 ESV) But you will receive power when the Holy Spirit has come upon you, and you will be my witnesses in Jerusalem and in all Judea and Samaria, and to the end of the earth."

(Psalm 42:5 ESV) Why are you cast down, O my soul, and why are you in turmoil within me? Hope in God; for I shall again praise him, my salvation

(2 Timothy 1:12 ESV) Which is why I suffer as I do. But I am not ashamed, for I know whom I have believed, and I am convinced that he is able to guard until that Day what has been entrusted to me.

(1 John 5:14-15 ESV) And this is the confidence that we have toward him, that if we ask anything according to his will he hears us. And if we know that he hears us in whatever we ask, we know that we have the requests that we have asked of him.

(Romans 8:32 ESV) He who did not spare his own Son but gave him up for us all, how will he not also with him graciously give us all things?

(Romans 8:30 ESV) And those whom he predestined he also called, and those whom he called he also justified, and those whom he justified he also glorified.

(Proverbs 3:26 ESV) For the Lord will be your confidence and will keep your foot from being caught.

(Hebrews 13:5 ESV) Keep your life free from love of money, and be content with what you have, for he has said, "I will never leave you nor forsake you."

(Jeremiah 1:6-9 ESV) Then I said, "Ah, Lord God! Behold, I do not know how to speak, for I am only a youth." But the Lord said to me, "Do not say, 'I am only a youth'; for to all to whom I send you, you shall go, and whatever I command you, you shall speak. Do not be afraid of them, for I am with you to deliver you, declares the Lord." Then the Lord put out his hand and touched my mouth. And the Lord said to me, "Behold, I have put my words in your mouth.

(Isaiah 41:10 ESV)Fear not, for I am with you; be not dismayed, for I am your God; I will strengthen you, I will help you, I will uphold you with my righteous right hand.

(Isaiah 40:31 ESV) But they who wait for the Lord shall renew their strength; they shall mount up with wings like eagles; they shall run and not be weary; they shall walk and not faint.

(Matthew 9:29 ESV) Then he touched their eyes, saying, "According to your faith be it done to you."

(Psalm 50:15 ESV) And call upon me in the day of trouble; I will deliver you, and you shall glorify me."

Joy

Proverbs 17:22 — A joyful heart is good medicine, but a crushed spirit dries up the bones. (ESV)

Joy is what God desires for his people. But unfortunately, we live in a world that does a better job at taking away joy than it does giving it. People that live a life full of joy age more gracefully than those that do not. Joy heals; it strengthens and mends broken hearts. People spend hours upon hours working a job or running a business so that they can buy a sense of joy or position themselves in a place where they can receive it. The benefit of being a believer is the fact that we do **not** have to work or earn joy. God promises it to us, and no one or nothing has the right to take it from us.

In Proverbs 17:22, Solomon teaches us that joy is like good medicine. Joy has healing power, not only for the body but the mind and spirit as well. An important point to understand is that God desires us to live a life full of joy (John 16:24). God understands that life can be difficult and stressful, but our hope is in Him. And in this hope we find joy! We can rejoice when the trials of life come our way. Why? Because we know that the trials that come cannot destroy us, but, instead, they teach us to be more patient, they teach us to preserve, and they help us to be transformed into the image and likeness of Jesus Christ (James 1:2-4). Our joy can and should be full every day, and this is one of the benefits of being a believer!

As you study the scriptures about joy, remember that God desires you to live a life full of joy. Do not allow people or circumstances to take away your joy. They didn't give you the joy, so they can't take it away. Speak the Word over your life daily, and meditate on the Scriptures so that your joy is full daily.

Do you walk in the fullness of joy that the Bible speaks of? What people or situations in your life do you allow to take away your joy?

Joy Scriptures

(Romans 12:12 ESV) Rejoice in hope, be patient in tribulation, be constant in prayer.

(Philippians 4:4 ESV) Rejoice in the Lord always; again I will say, Rejoice.

(Galatians 5:22 ESV) But the fruit of the Spirit is love, joy, peace, patience, kindness, goodness, faithfulness,

(1 Peter 1:8 ESV) Though you have not seen him, you love him. Though you do not now see him, you believe in him and rejoice with joy that is inexpressible and filled with glory,

(Romans 15:13 ESV) May the God of hope fill you with all joy and peace in believing, so that by the power of the Holy Spirit you may abound in hope.

(John 16:24 ESV) Until now you have asked nothing in my name. Ask, and you will receive, that your joy may be full.

(Psalm 16:9 ESV) Therefore my heart is glad, and my whole being rejoices; my flesh also dwells secure.

(1 Thessalonians 5:16 ESV) Rejoice always,

(John 16:22 ESV) So also you have sorrow now, but I will see you again, and your hearts will rejoice, and no one will take your joy from you.

(James 1:2-4 ESV) Count it all joy, my brothers, when you meet trials of various kinds, for you know that the testing of your faith produces steadfastness. And let steadfastness have its full effect, that you may be perfect and complete, lacking in nothing.

(Proverbs 10:28 ESV) The hope of the righteous brings joy, but the expectation of the wicked will perish.

(Luke 15:10 ESV) Just so, I tell you, there is joy before the angels of God over one sinner who repents."

(1 Peter 4:13 ESV) But rejoice insofar as you share Christ's sufferings, that you may also rejoice and be glad when his glory is revealed.

(Romans 5:11 ESV) More than that, we also rejoice in God through our Lord Jesus Christ, through whom we have now received reconciliation.

(Isaiah 55:12 ESV) "For you shall go out in joy and be led forth in peace; the mountains and the hills before you shall break forth into singing, and all the trees of the field shall clap their hands.

(1 John 1:4 ESV) And we are writing these things so that our joy may be complete.

(2 Corinthians 8:2 ESV) For in a severe test of affliction, their abundance of joy and their extreme poverty have overflowed in a wealth of generosity on their part.

(Proverbs 17:22 ESV) A joyful heart is good medicine, but a crushed spirit dries up the bones.

(Colossians 1:11 ESV) May you be strengthened with all power, according to his glorious might, for all endurance and patience with joy,

(Jeremiah 29:11 ESV) For I know the plans I have for you, declares the Lord, plans for welfare and not for evil, to give you a future and a hope.

(Psalm 33:21 ESV) For our heart is glad in him, because we trust in his holy name.

(Psalm 30:5 ESV) For his anger is but for a moment, and his favor is for a lifetime. Weeping may tarry for the night, but joy comes with the morning.

(Psalm 118:24 ESV) This is the day that the Lord has made; let us rejoice and be glad in it.

(Psalm 100:1 ESV) A Psalm for giving thanks. Make a joyful noise to the Lord, all the earth!

(Psalm 150:6 ESV) Let everything that has breath praise the Lord! Praise the Lord!

(Psalm 28:7 ESV) The Lord is my strength and my shield; in him my heart trusts, and I am helped; my heart exults, and with my song I give thanks to him.

(Jude 1:24 ESV) Now to him who is able to keep you from stumbling and to present you blameless before the presence of his glory with great joy,.

(Psalm 126:5 ESV) Those who sow in tears shall reap with shouts of joy!

Wisdom & Knowledge

Psalm 111:10 — The fear of the LORD is the beginning of wisdom; all those who practice it have a good

understanding. His praise endures forever! (ESV)

Wisdom and knowledge are sought after by many, whether it's a student that will spend years in school to acquire it or whether it's a company looking to gain a competitive advantage in their industry through acquiring more advanced knowledge about their product or service. Wisdom and knowledge are needed to have success in life. The Bible talks in depth about the need for a person to acquire as much wisdom and knowledge as possible. The problem that many people face in today's day and age is trying to figure out what is wisdom and what is not. All over the Internet, people promise that they are experts or gurus on everything from diets, real estate, marriage, or life in general. With so many vying for our attention, it is important to distinguish between what is truth and what is a lie!

The Bible tells us in Psalms 111:10 that the beginning of wisdom is the fear of the Lord. The word fear in the verse is not the English word we commonly use as fear, which means to be scared or afraid of. The word here means to "reverence." So, the reverence of God or the acknowledgement of God for who He is, this is the beginning of wisdom. When you and I accepted Jesus Christ as our Lord and Savior, we took the first step in reverencing the Lord. We took the first step towards wisdom!

Throughout the Old and New Testaments, we see God's desire to reveal Himself to us and to teach us about His principles for success in life. The entire books of Proverbs and Ecclesiastics were written by Solomon. He was the wisest man to walk the earth outside of Christ. Solomon dedicated his life to giving us proper knowledge with correct understanding that leads to wisdom. *Wisdom is applied understanding of correct knowledge.* We can **only** walk in wisdom when we have correct knowledge and have a proper understanding of that knowledge. This is why the Bible says that the fear of the Lord is the beginning of wisdom. Why? Because if you do not know the creator of life, you will **never** know or understand the purpose of life or how to live in it properly. The benefit of being a believer is that we have taken the first step, and our Heavenly Father is waiting to reveal to us all the mysteries of life (Ephesians 3:1-6 and Matthew 13:10-11).

As you study the scriptures on wisdom and knowledge, seek the Lord in prayer to give you proper understanding of the verses you study. Meditate on the Word daily and always look for areas in your life to apply your understanding of the knowledge of God's word in wisdom.

Do you live by the wisdom and knowledge of the Lord? Or do you depend on your own wisdom and knowledge? In what areas of your life can you walk in God's wisdom better?

Wisdom & Knowledge Scriptures

(James 1:5 ESV) If any of you lacks wisdom, let him ask God, who gives generously to all without reproach, and it will be given him.

(Proverbs 1:7 ESV) The fear of the Lord is the beginning of knowledge; fools despise wisdom and instruction.

(Psalm 111:10 ESV) The fear of the Lord is the beginning of wisdom; all those who practice it have a good understanding. His praise endures forever!

(Ecclesiastes 7:12 ESV) For the protection of wisdom is like the protection of money, and the advantage of knowledge is that wisdom preserves the life of him who has it.

(1 Corinthians 3:19-20 ESV) For the wisdom of this world is folly with God. For it is written, "He catches the wise in their craftiness," and again, "The Lord knows the thoughts of the wise, that they are futile."

(1 Timothy 2:4 ESV) Who desires all people to be saved and to come to the knowledge of the truth.

(Colossians 2:8 ESV) See to it that no one takes you captive by philosophy and empty deceit, according to human tradition, according to the elemental spirits of the world, and not according to Christ.

(Isaiah 11:2 ESV) And the Spirit of the Lord shall rest upon him, the Spirit of wisdom and understanding, the Spirit of counsel and might, the Spirit of knowledge and the fear of the Lord.

(1 Corinthians 1:20 ESV) Where is the one who is wise? Where is the scribe? Where is the debater of this age? Has not God made foolish the wisdom of the world?

(Matthew 7:7-8 ESV) "Ask, and it will be given to you; seek, and you will find; knock, and it will be opened to you. For everyone who asks receives, and the one who seeks finds, and to the one who knocks it will be opened.

(2 Chronicles 1:7-12 ESV) In that night God appeared to Solomon, and said to him, "Ask what I shall give you." [8] And Solomon said to God, "You have shown great and steadfast love to David my father, and have made me king in his place. [9] O LORD God, let your word to David my father be now fulfilled, for you have made me king over a people as numerous as the dust of the earth. [10] Give me now wisdom and knowledge to go out and come in before this people, for who can govern this people of yours, which is so great?" [11] God answered Solomon, "Because this was in your heart, and you have not asked for possessions, wealth, honor, or the life of those who hate you, and have not even asked for long life, but have asked for wisdom and knowledge for yourself that you may govern my people over whom I have made you king,[12] wisdom and knowledge are granted to you. I will also give you riches, possessions, and honor, such as none of the kings had who were before you, and none after you shall have the like."

(Romans 1:22-25 ESV) Claiming to be wise, they became fools, and exchanged the glory of the immortal God for images resembling mortal man and birds and animals and creeping things. Therefore God gave them up in the lusts of their hearts to impurity, to the dishonoring of their bodies among themselves, because they exchanged the truth about God for a lie and worshiped and served the creature rather than the Creator, who is blessed forever! Amen.

(Proverbs 20:15 ESV) There is gold and abundance of costly stones, but the lips of knowledge are a precious jewel.

(1 John 4:18 ESV) here is no fear in love, but perfect love casts out fear. For fear has to do with punishment, and whoever fears has not been perfected in love.

Praise & Worship

Psalm 150:6 — Let everything that has breath praise the LORD! Praise the LORD! (ESV)

When someone receives praise, they did something to deserve it. They helped someone or something in a positive way, thus resulting in their praise. If we can give men praise for what they do, how much more can we give God our praise for all that He has done for us? God created us and He sustains us throughout our lives, and this why we should praise Him. The Bible says that everything that has breath should praise the Lord (Psalm 150:6).

Our praise and worship of God reveals our faith and dependence on Him. The Bible tells us that our faith is what pleases God (Hebrews 11:6). Our worship acknowledges Him as our Lord and our reverence to His will. The Bible says that God inhabits the praise of His people (Psalm 22:3). The Bible teaches us that God reveals Himself to those who seek Him, and one of the easiest ways we can seek God is through our praise and worship time. Jesus taught us that God is a Spirit, and when we worship God, we must worship Him in spirit and in truth (John 4:24). We must worship God with the correct attitude and in the truth of who He is. Our worship towards God should be genuine and stems from the true knowledge of who He is. It is a popular belief that says, "When praises go up, blessings come down." While this is an encouraging statement, there is no direct biblical verse that states this. The Bible says we **are** blessed, and because of this fact, we give God our praise and worship. Our praise and worship are a sign that we acknowledge the fact that we are blessed. So we do not have to praise God to receive His blessings—we **already** have it!

As you study the scriptures on praise and worship, remember that you are already blessed and your praise and worship acknowledge this fact. Meditate on the Word daily, and speak it over your life. Every day you should praise and worship God, because He is worthy of it. As believers, we have the benefit of worshipping the true and living God who brings us freedom.

Do you praise and worship God on a daily basis?

Praise & Worship Scripture

(Psalm 150:1-6 ESV) Praise the LORD! Praise God in his sanctuary; praise him in his mighty heavens! [2] Praise him for his mighty deeds; praise him according to his excellent greatness! [3] Praise him with trumpet sound; praise him with lute and harp! [4] Praise him with tambourine and dance; praise him with strings and pipe! [5] Praise him with sounding cymbals; praise him with loud clashing cymbals! [6] Let everything that has breath praise the LORD! Praise the LORD!

(Psalm 100:2 ESV) Serve the Lord with gladness! Come into his presence with singing!

(John 4:23 ESV) But the hour is coming, and is now here, when the true worshipers will worship the Father in spirit and truth, for the Father is seeking such people to worship him.

(Psalm 150:6 ESV) Let everything that has breath praise the Lord! Praise the Lord!

(Colossians 3:16 ESV) Let the word of Christ dwell in you richly, teaching and admonishing one another in all wisdom, singing psalms and hymns and spiritual songs, with thankfulness in your hearts to God.

(Hebrews 13:15 ESV) Through him then let us continually offer up a sacrifice of praise to God, that is, the fruit of lips that acknowledge his name.

(Psalm 95:1-6 ESV) Oh come, let us sing to the LORD; let us make a joyful noise to the rock of our salvation! [2] Let us come into his presence with thanksgiving; let us make a joyful noise to him with songs of praise! [3] For the LORD is a great God, and a great King above all gods. [4] In his hand are the depths of the earth; the heights of the mountains are his also. [5] The sea is his, for he made it, and his hands formed the dry land. [6] Oh come, let us worship and bow down; let us kneel before the LORD, our Maker!

(Psalm 117:1-2 ESV) Praise the Lord, all nations! Extol him, all peoples! For great is his steadfast love toward us, and the faithfulness of the Lord endures forever. Praise the Lord!

(Psalm 100:4 ESV) Enter his gates with thanksgiving, and his courts with praise! Give thanks to him; bless his name!

(Ephesians 5:19 ESV) Addressing one another in psalms and hymns and spiritual songs, singing and making melody to the Lord with your heart,

(Zephaniah 3:17 ESV) The Lord your God is in your midst, a mighty one who will save; he will rejoice over you with gladness; he will quiet you by his love; he will exult over you with loud singing.

(Psalm 96:1-9 ESV) Oh sing to the LORD a new song; sing to the LORD, all the earth! ² Sing to the LORD, bless his name; tell of his salvation from day to day. ³ Declare his glory among the nations, his marvelous works among all the peoples! ⁴ For great is the LORD, and greatly to be praised; he is to be feared above all gods. ⁵ For all the gods of the peoples are worthless idols, but the LORD made the heavens. ⁶ Splendor and majesty are before him; strength and beauty are in his sanctuary. ⁷ Ascribe to the LORD, O families of the peoples, ascribe to the LORD glory and strength! ⁸ Ascribe to the LORD the glory due his name; bring an offering, and come into his courts! ⁹ Worship the LORD in the splendor of holiness; tremble before him, all the earth!

(Psalm 30:11 ESV) You have turned for me my mourning into dancing; you have loosed my sackcloth and clothed me with gladness,

(John 4:24 ESV) God is spirit, and those who worship him must worship in spirit and truth."

(Psalm 146:1-2 ESV) Praise the Lord! Praise the Lord, O my soul! I will praise the Lord as long as I live; I will sing praises to my God while I have my being.

(Psalm 149:3 ESV) Let them praise his name with dancing, making melody to him with tambourine and lyre!

(Psalm 22:3 ESV) Yet you are holy, enthroned on the praises of Israel.

(Psalm 33:2-3 ESV) Give thanks to the Lord with the lyre; make melody to him with the harp of ten strings! Sing to him a new song; play skillfully on the strings, with loud shouts.

(Psalm 34:1 ESV) Of David, when he changed his behavior before Abimelech, so that he drove him out, and he went away. I will bless the Lord at all times; his praise shall continually be in my mouth.

(1 Chronicles 13:8 ESV) And David and all Israel were rejoicing before God with all their might, with song and lyres and harps and tambourines and cymbals and trumpets.

ABOUT THE AURTHOR

Terell Ward is a husband
and father. Terell is the
Pastor of The Word in
Action Church – Phoenix
AZ. He has been in
ministry since he was 15
years old. The
motivational speaker and
pastor is truly dedicated to
building the Kingdom of
God.

www.ingramcontent.com/pod-product-compliance
Lightning Source LLC
Chambersburg PA
CBHW072201090426
42740CB00012B/2336